ABOUT GANESHA PRESS

Ganesha Press is the publishing house of Dechen, an international association of Sakya and Kagyu Buddhist centres and groups founded by Lama Jampa Thaye under the authority of Karma Thinley Rinpoche.

Dispelling the Darkness of Suffering

A Concise Word Commentary on
the Seven Points of Mind Training
of the Mahayana

theg.pa.chen.po'i.blo.sbyong.don.bdun.ma'i.tshig.'grel.
mdor.bsdus.sdug.bsngal.mun.sel.zhes.bya.ba.bzhugs.so

Karma Thinley Rinpoche

Translated by Dan Hore

Dispelling the Darkness of Suffering

Illustrations of Maitreya, Atisha and the Stupa of Enlightenment by Rana Lister

This edition by Rabsel Publications in partnership with Ganesha Press and Dechen Foundation Books.

Ganesha Press
121 Sommerville Road, St Andrews, Bristol, BS6 5BX, UK

Rabsel Publications
16, rue de Babylone
76430 La Remuée, France
www.rabsel.com
contact@rabsel.com

ISBN 978-2-36017-053-1

Karma Thinley Rinpoche

Contents

Foreword ... 3
Translator's Preface ... 5

Dispelling the Darkness of Suffering ... 7
1. The Preliminaries: Showing the Foundation of the Dharma ... 11
2. The Main Practice: Training in Bodhichitta ... 13
3. The Transformation of Adverse Conditions into the Path of Awakening ... 27
4. Showing How to Implement the Practice for a Whole Lifetime ... 39
5. The Measure of Mind Training ... 45
6. Pledges of Mind Training ... 49
7. Precepts of Mind Training ... 57
Additional Instructions from the Lineage ... 69
Conclusion ... 75

Biography of Karma Thinley Rinpoche ... 79
The Tibetan Text ... 83

Foreword

Over the centuries one of the most celebrated cycles of Mahayana meditation instructions has been *The Seven Points of Mind Training*, which was elaborated in its definitive form by Geshe Chekhawa Yeshe Dorje (1102–1176). Essentially a crystallization of teachings brought to Tibet in the mid-eleventh century by the Indian pandita Atisha (979–1053), this contemplative system embodies the methods by which the awakened mind of boundless affection for all beings and profound insight into reality can be generated.

Originally transmitted in the early Kadam tradition, the principal repository of the lineages of Atisha, the *Seven Points* has inspired commentaries by such luminaries as Geshe Se Chilbupa, Thogme Zangpo, Shamar Konchok Yenlak and Jamgon Kongtrul Lodro Thaye. Now I am delighted to introduce this new commentary, entitled *Dispelling The Darkness of Suffering*, recently composed by my master Karma Thinley Rinpoche.

Rinpoche's connection with Kadam dharma is profound and extensive. Already in Tibet he received many Kadampa teachings from masters such as Khangsar

Khenpo and Drupon Sanjay Phuntsok, while subsequently in India he obtained Kadam teachings from Ling Rinpoche, Trijang Rinpoche and Kalu Rinpoche. In fact, it was from Kalu Rinpoche that he received the entire set of Kadam transmissions contained in Kongtrul's monumental *Treasury of Spiritual Instructions*. Such an education and training make Rinpoche a worthy successor to his eminent predecessors as a commentator on *The Seven Points*.

Dispelling The Darkness of Suffering presents a wonderfully clear account of how mind training (in Tibetan, lojong) is to be practised both in formal sessions of meditation and in everyday situations. Drawing upon a rich variety of sources and his own mastery of the system, Rinpoche makes its methods of practice extraordinarily accessible so that we will be well equipped to give rise to the timeless qualities of wisdom and compassion.

I would like to commend Dan Hore for his work in bringing this translation of Rinpoche's beautiful commentary to fruition. It is also a pleasure to acknowledge all the assistance given by Tulku Konchog Tenzin and Kunga Gyaltsen in this endeavour.

Lama Jampa Thaye

Translator's Preface

I wish to thank Lama Karma Thinley Rinpoche for his very kind and illuminating responses to my questions concerning the Tibetan, Lama Jampa Thaye for his substantial guidance and encouragement, and Khenpo Tulku Konchog Tenzin for his numerous suggestions and clarifications. I must also acknowledge and thank Kunga Gyaltsen for many helpful discussions and comments, as well as Adrian O'Sullivan for input into early drafts, and Dolma Gutmann for clarifying some points of Tibetan. Thanks also to Benjamin Lister for his skilful editing work in the preparation of the final text.

I apologize wholeheartedly to Rinpoche, and to all readers, for any errors or omissions within the translation.

In accord with tradition, the transmission of this Buddhist dharma text is only complete when one has received, at least, the *lung* (reading transmission) from a qualified Mahayana teacher.

Geshe Chekhawa

Dispelling the Darkness of Suffering

Om Svasti

The dense clouds of compassion gather in the sky of knowledge.
Through the power of the gentle rain of their sublime activity,
A lotus garden of benefit and happiness flourishes for countless beings.
To the matchless supreme guide, Lord of the Shakyas, I pay homage.

A stream of compassionate blessings, like a rosary of pearls,
Flows from the pollen heart of the lotus held by the Thousand-eyed One.
Lama Chenrezig, who dispels the torment of beings,
I place your jewelled feet with devotion at the crown of my head.

Mind training is the excellent essence of the nectar of the Mahayana,
And since good fortune increases merely by repeating the words
Even without the innate power of its authentic meditation,
I will labour at these annotations in order to aid my own recollection.

Having composed these virtuous lines, an auspicious scattering of small flowers to the holy ones, I will set out the division of these brief notes on the *Seven Points of Mind Training*. These instructions for taking negative conditions onto the path were composed by the holder of the great injunction of bodhichitta, Geshe Chekhawa Yeshe Dorje, for all practitioners of the holy dharma in this dark age:

The Preliminaries: Showing the Foundations of the Dharma
The Main Practice: Training in Bodhichitta
Transforming Adverse Conditions into the Path of Awakening
Showing How to Implement the Practice for a Lifetime
The Measure of Mind Training
Pledges of Mind Training
Precepts of Mind Training

If one wishes to learn the detailed history of the mind training[1] lineage, together with the extensive instructions, these can be found in the major commentaries, such as the excellent *Path to Enlightenment*. Here is a brief summary:

The essence nectar of the pith instructions is a transmission from Serlingpa.

The profound pith instructions of the mind training of the exchange of self and other were transmitted from

1 Tibetan: blo sbyong ('lojong')

the supreme teacher to Lord Maitreya, and then through an unbroken lineage to the three: Lord Serlingpa[2], Guru Dharmarakshita, who by the practice of loving-kindness, compassion and mind training was able to give away his own flesh to the hungry, and Guru Maitriyogin, who had the power to absorb the sufferings of beings.

In general, seventy-two gurus bestowed sutra and mantra teachings upon Lord Atisha, and principal among these were these three who transmitted the mind training instructions. Furthermore, when Atisha uttered the names of his other teachers, he joined his palms together at his heart, but when he exclaimed Serlingpa's name he joined them at the crown of his head in boundless devotion, and tears fell from his eyes. When asked the reason for this, Atisha replied: 'This bodhichitta of exchanging self for other is the result of Serlingpa's kindness.'

From the time of his arrival in Tibet, Atisha turned the wheel of dharma in the same way, and continued Lord Serlingpa's tradition of the profound mind training. The lineage then passed by degrees to Chekhawa Yeshe Dorje, the author of the *Seven Points of Mind Training*.

> **The main topic of the text is to be understood in accord with the examples of the diamond, the sun and the supreme tree.**

The precious diamond surpasses in splendour those other precious gems that overcome and dispel poverty, the light of the sun surpasses in splendour those other lights that overcome and dispel darkness, and the supreme medicinal tree surpasses in splendour those other trees and herbs that overcome and dispel sickness. In accord with these examples, bodhichitta surpasses in splendour those other dharmas that dispel suffering and accomplish benefit and bliss. By these three examples, the excellence of the profound mind training teachings is demonstrated.

---

2 Serlingpa's name in Sanskrit is Suvarṇadvīpa Dharmakirti

> **At this time of increase in the five degenerations, this is the method by which to transform them into the path to enlightenment.**

This means that in this present age of strife, the power of the five degenerations is extremely great, and undesirable negative conditions are difficult to surmount by means of other dharmas. However, through the methods of mind training, they can be transformed into the path of enlightenment. This is explained in detail in the main part below.

All three vehicles contain skilful means for training the mind. However, the general term 'mind training' has a specific designation here, and signifies the instructions for exchanging self and other derived from the lineage of Serlingpa. The main part of the text **begins** with the **training in the preliminaries.**

Point One

The Preliminaries: Showing the Foundation of the Dharma

If you wish to meditate on this practice of mind training in a single session, **begin** with the **preliminary teachings**. The place where you practise should be very clean and arrayed with beautiful offerings if you have them. Seated comfortably on a cushion, recite the *Seven Branch Prayer* well, then **train** in the motivations common to the greater and lesser vehicles. These include the difficulty of finding the freedoms and endowments; death and impermanence; karma–cause and result; and the defects of samsara. Clearly recollecting these, turn your mind towards the dharma.

Atisha

Point Two

The Main Practice: Training in Bodhichitta

Then, having taken refuge and recited the four immeasurables, generate the uncommon bodhichittas of aspiration and application as follows.

> **In order to quickly benefit all sentient beings, I must attain the level of a completely perfect buddha. For this reason I will train in the profound instructions of the mind training of the Mahayana.**
>
> Recite this three times.

To meditate upon the actual guru, or upon the sacred appearance of the noble Padmapani, the embodiment of the compassion of all the conquerors, is called 'excellent'. Therefore, visualize one's root guru as actually present in the form of noble Chenrezig upon a lotus and moon disc at the crown of one's head. White light rays shine from his body, pervading space, and he regards beings with a mind[3] of unobjectified compassion. Think that he is the essence of all objects of refuge, which are gathered together in him, and supplicate the mind training lineage. In particular, recite:

---

3 thugs (pron. 'tuk'): the mind or heart of a buddha

Great spiritual master, completely perfect guru, bless me that exceptional loving-kindness, compassion and bodhichitta arise within my mind stream.

Recite this up to 100,000 times.

Also, recite the supplication to Atisha composed by Dromtonpa:

Most wondrous and excellent ocean of glory,
Bless me to perfect bodhichitta for all beings.

Descended from a royal lineage and learned in the five sciences,
You travelled to the glorious Land of Snows in accordance with a prophecy of Tara,
And, holding others dearer than yourself, accomplished their benefit.
Incomparable Atisha, I supplicate you.

Please bless me in this very moment
And dispel the suffering of beings right now.
Establish all beings on the true path of enlightenment,
And bestow the source of all benefit and bliss.

May happiness begin right now;
Bestow the source of bliss this very day.
May all the sufferings of samsara be defeated.
May all obstacles to dharma be averted.

Bless me so that my activity is never apart from dharma.

Make this supplication from the core of one's heart until a fierce devotion has arisen. Following this, Lama Chenrezig descends through the aperture of Brahma at the crown of one's head. Clear and smiling, he dwells upon a lotus and moon seat within a pavilion of light in the centre of one's heart. Think that his mind and one's own mind are undifferentiated, and rest for a moment in equanimity.

Begin all sessions in this way. Concerning this meditation on the lama, Geshe Chilbupa's *Guru Yoga of Mind Training* says:

> Even if a student possesses virtue, diligence and so on, realisation will not be attained without relying upon a guru who is a source of blessings. Therefore it is essential to rely upon an excellent guru. Regarding the characteristics of such a guru: 'To be a lineage holder is a defining characteristic, but, if realisation is present, he or she is completely qualified.'
>
> One should rely upon a lineage of transmission of bodhichitta, descending from the perfect Buddha, which is stable and certain. Such is the transmission from Lord Atisha. The 'reliance through the door of the meaning' is to accomplish through the three gates whatever has been imparted by the guru. The 'reliance through the door of secret symbols'[4] is to visualize the guru at one's heart centre or at the crown of one's head, and to supplicate him or her with devotion.

Subsequently, hold the body straight and focus on the inhalation and exhalation of the breath. Breathe naturally and count the out-breaths up to twenty-one. By leaving mind and breath in their natural state, become a suitable vessel for meditative absorption.

Then, follow the words and meaning of the main practice step by step, and meditate on these in order to decisively tame your own continuum.

Meditation on the Bodhichitta of Ultimate Truth

The Main Practice: Analytical Meditation and Even Settling

Analytical Meditation

First, externally apprehended objects are established not to be truly existent.

4 the Vajrayana

Consider phenomena to be like dreams.

Apparent **phenomena**, the objects of the six senses, are not established as truly existent, being nothing more than projections resulting from the positive and negative actions of each individual being. **Think** these phenomena **to be** just **like** the beings and environment within a **dream**, which on waking are understood to be illusions lacking any reality. Determine to train in this time and again.

This being so, it might be wondered whether the perceiving mind – that which is confused in regard to external objects – itself possesses true existence.

Investigate the nature of unborn awareness.

When this mind is investigated, it too is discovered to lack true existence. At first, there is no point at which it arises, therefore it is **unborn**. In the middle, it does not abide anywhere, either inside or outside the body. Finally, there is no place where mind ceases. This **investigation into** the essence **of awareness**, which is just the unity of clarity and emptiness, will establish certainty in its **nature** being unelaborated emptiness, like space.

If recognition of the remedy, the conceiving of emptiness in the emptiness of mind, arises at this point:

Even the remedy is naturally self-liberated.

Even the remedy itself, mindfulness of the recognition of emptiness, **is naturally self-liberated** for the meditator in a state free from objectification. Settle without distraction in the wisdom that does not objectify the three circles.

Settling Meditation

Rest in the state of the alaya, the essence.

Rest free of sinking and scattering **in this** non-conceptual **state**, the luminous natural **essence** of the **alaya**, the original nature untarnished by discriminations of good or bad.

As Jetsun Mila says:

> To identify the alaya – the empty and luminous mind of all of us sentient beings, untainted by any fault or quality of samsara or nirvana whatsoever – it is known as 'Buddha, the ground-of-all (alaya)'. It is that which recognises its own nature, the primordial wisdom of awareness.

This completes the settling meditation, in which one continues to **settle** during sessions of the main practice.

Ultimate Bodhichitta: The Subsequent Stage

Between sessions, see everything as illusory.

Between sessions, whether eating, sleeping, walking or sitting, transform all everyday activity into the path while resting within meditative awareness. Without forgetting this, relinquish clinging to **everything** – self, other, the world and the beings within it – as real. It is all **illusory**, appearing without truly existing. Bring this onto the path.

MEDITATION ON THE BODHICHITTA OF RELATIVE TRUTH

The Main Practice: Sending and Taking (Tonglen)

The object of this meditation is all sentient beings, who are afflicted by suffering. We recognize each to have been our mother, and remember their kindness with gratitude.

First reflect on the kindness of one's present mother, then widen this out to encompass all other beings. Having developed an uncontrived sense that all beings have previously been one's mother, from a state of loving-kindness and compassion towards them:

Practise sending and taking alternately. Place these two upon the breath.

Since the bodhichitta of exchanging self and other is the essence of mind training, we **send** all of our happiness and virtue gathered throughout the three times, together with our belongings and enjoyment of physical comforts, to other sentient beings, and **take** all of their sufferings, both causes and results, for ourselves without remainder. **These two** visualizations should be **practised in alternation**, by **placing** this very happiness and suffering **upon** the **flow** of one's **breath**.

To meditate on this, breathe in the negative deeds, obscurations and sufferings of all beings together as black air, which enters through one's nostrils and pores and then dissolves into one's self-clinging, located in the heart centre.

If one meditates upon oneself as a yidam such as Chenrezig, visualize that the black air is absorbed into the clear appearance of the deity. Chenrezig then shines with brilliant white light, like sunlight striking the side of a snow mountain. Generate immeasurable compassion, and think that the misdeeds of all sentient beings of the six classes are purified, and that each becomes free from whatever sufferings they have.

Next, as one breathes out through one's nostrils and pores, white light goes out to the realms and physical forms of each being of the six classes and is absorbed into them. Through this, all of one's virtue and happiness becomes a vast and inexhaustible treasury of space, and each obtains whatever they need. Think that, free of suffering, they enjoy happiness and well-being in body and mind until proceeding to the state of buddhahood. In this way, generate limitless loving-kindness.

This is the actual practice for regular meditation sessions. The same attitude should be applied in the post-meditative state. It is said that sending and taking is practised because it is easy to focus the mind, it ensures that the training is swift, and it subdues numerous concepts.

It is also the essence of the four immeasurables: sending is immeasurable loving-kindness; taking is immeasurable compassion; to visualize the dispelling of all beings' suffering and their establishment in happiness is immeasurable joy; and its impartial cultivation towards friends and enemies alike is immeasurable equanimity.

Question: 'Might not taking the suffering of others bring harm to me?' One way to answer this is by considering those such as Geshe Chekhawa, who have mastered the exceptional bodhichitta of the exchange of self and other, and in whom self-clinging has become completely exhausted. Shantideva said:

> They will even enter the Avichi hell,
> Like geese plunging into a lotus lake.

They have accepted others' suffering and wish to experience it, and having perfected the special practice of sending and taking, would gladly experience all of this suffering in a single moment for the sake of their happiness.

However, it may be understood through scripture that the ripening of a negative action performed by any being of the six classes can only be experienced through the skandhas[5] of the doer of that same action. The result cannot be transferred to another.

Furthermore, when the previous buddhas practised sending and taking, they never experienced the sins, obscurations or sufferings of other beings within their own bodies. Yet, through the heart of compassion engendered by the practice they traversed the five paths and ten bhumis, and attained ultimate enlightenment. It is said that we too, through the skilful means of great compassion, can attain to this state. The essence of these is the meditation of sending and taking.

---

5 The five skandhas ('heaps' or 'aggregates') are form, feeling, perception, constructs and consciousness, the five psychophysical constituents that make up body and mind

Manjushri Sakya Pandita says:

Some say that the bodhichitta of exchange
Is not a suitable object of meditation.

Think of it this way.
Examine whether the bodhichitta of exchanging self and other
Is virtuous or non-virtuous.
If it is virtuous,
This is inconsistent with its giving rise to suffering.

If non-virtuous, the action of exchanging
Must arise from the three poisons.
This exchange cannot come from the three poisons.
This being so, how can suffering arise?

Not all prayers of the mind training of the bodhisattvas
Are unlimited in their effects.
If they had such force,
Maitrakanyaka's head would be in agony forever.

Even the buddhas of the three times,
Because they cultivate the exchange of self and other,
Would experience continual suffering,
And all those beings they exchange with
Would endure no samsaric suffering.

Therefore, words such as these
Should be known as the counsel of Mara.

The exchange of self and other is said to be
The heart of the Buddha's doctrine.

Therefore, since this practice is in accordance with the words of Lama Manjugosha, practise with joy.

During the main practice in formal sessions, endeavour in the absorptions of calm abiding[6] and insight[7] and make a special effort in sending and taking. If you practise Tangtong Gyalpo's meditation and recitation of Chenrezig, the *Benefit of Beings that Pervades Space*, unite the recitation of the six syllables and the visualisation with sending and taking.

Conclude with short or extensive mind training aspiration prayers, as appropriate, and seal the session with prayers and dedications, such as the *Aspiration Prayer of Good Conduct*. This completes the section concerning the practice of mind training in formal sessions.

Relative Bodhichitta: The Subsequent Stage

In the post-meditation phase, between sessions, always repeat phrases such as the following. This will help one truly to apply the teachings in practice.

Three objects, three poisons, three roots of virtue.

Longing, covetousness, avarice, the desire to steal, and so on in respect of **objects**, material things or sentient beings, that are attractive to us, is desire-attachment.

Likewise, anger, malice, rancour, lying, slander, harsh speech and wrong views in regard to objects that repel us, such as enemies and demons, is hatred.

A mind of no harm or benefit at all towards beings, objects, and so on that are neutral to us, while within that state of indifference there remains grasping at existence, is ignorance.

Recognise these **three** to be like **three poisonous** substances, roots that produce suffering for oneself and others, and eliminate them as far as possible by using this

6 Skt. shamatha
7 Skt. vipashyana

method from the *Direct Path to Enlightenment* to transform them into **three roots** of **virtue**.

> Whenever desire arises, think: **'May all the defilements of desire of every sentient being be gathered into this. May they all gain the root of virtue of freedom from desire. Now that their defilements are overcome, may they remain free from them until buddhahood.'**
>
> Do the same when hatred arises: **'May all the defilements of hatred of every sentient being be gathered into this. May they all gain the root of virtue of freedom from hatred. Now that their defilements are overcome, may they remain free from them until buddhahood.'**
>
> And when ignorance arises: **'May all defilements of ignorance of every sentient being be gathered into this. May they all gain the root of virtue of freedom from ignorance. Now that their defilements are overcome, may they remain free from them until buddhahood.'**

By thinking or reciting these words with a virtuous attitude, the afflictions of the three poisons will be transformed by the path of sending and taking into three vast roots of virtue. The same goes for the defilements of pride, jealousy, avarice and so on. If they are redirected in this manner at the moment of their arising, it is excellent, like the transformation of a heap of rotting food, excrement and urine into manure, which when spread over a field will produce a good harvest.

Guru Rinpoche said:

> Whatever thoughts based on the five poisons arise,
> The flickering motion of mental objects, meet them first.
> Do not engage in contrived mental analysis afterwards.
> Thought's activity left in its natural state is liberated into the dharmakaya.

Without accepting or rejecting, leave things just as they are, in their natural state. This method to transform mental activity into primordial wisdom is an essential key point.

For encouragement and as an aid to mindfulness:

In all of your conduct train by means of phrases.

While eating, sleeping, walking or sitting – in **all of your conduct** – **train** by quietly reciting or chanting **phrases**.

Whatever is suffered by beings,
May all of it ripen in me.
May the bodhisattva sangha
Bring happiness to all beings.

When happy, may I dedicate all to others:
May space be filled with well-being and joy.
When unhappy, may I bear the suffering of all:
May the ocean of suffering dry up.

And:

May the misdeeds of others ripen in me,
And may all my virtue ripen for them.

And:

Whoever desires swift protection
For themselves and others
Should practise the holy secret
Of exchanging self and other.

These are the words of Conqueror's son Shantideva. It is said that 'holy secret' indicates the need to practise the key points of the sublime intent in a hidden way, since there is no room for it in the minds of trainees of little understanding, and they do not take even the least delight in difficult work. In another sense, 'holy secret' is the recognition that sending and taking, and ultimate truth, are both held to be bodhichitta. Je Rinpoche says:

Having generated the pure aspiration within my mind stream,
This bodhichitta that cultivates cherishing others over self,
May the level of unsurpassed enlightenment be bestowed.

As you recite the words of the holy ones, firmly recollect their meaning.

Begin the sequence of exchange with oneself.

Although the practice in its proper **sequence** is concerned with **exchange** with the sufferings of others, in order to become accustomed to this, **begin** by taking on **your own** suffering.

Think that all of the suffering one has experienced up until now, and will experience in future lifetimes, together with its causes, is gathered into this present body, and gathers and ripens upon this mind of self-cherishing. Due to this, grasping at 'I', 'mine' and so on – the groundless confusion of unawareness – is smashed into dust, and the wisdom of non-self is realised. It is said that any qualities attained through this purification should be used to help us take suffering from others.

'This being the case, is there any reason to care for oneself?' Consider the following. Self, or ego, that which functions as the ground of suffering, has no existence whatsoever. Yet, by clinging to and cherishing it, we accumulate various actions based on attachment and aversion, from which all the suffering of the world arises. Therefore it is vital to abandon self-clinging.

However, this body of ours is the fruit of the previous accumulation of merit, and, when used in the service of the holy dharma, it is an excellent support for liberation. For this reason, we should value it and look after it with food, clothing, medicine and so on. This being said, since we have given our body away to sentient beings, there is no reason to cling to self.

As Shantideva says:

Having freely given this body
For the welfare of all sentient beings,
They may beat it and the like as they please.
For what reason should I cherish it?

Point Three

The Transformation of Adverse Conditions into the Path of Awakening

> **When the world and its inhabitants are full of negativity, transform negative circumstances into the path of enlightenment.**

When the wealth of the world's external **environment** is damaged by harms from the four elements, and deteriorates due to the effects of man-made toxins and so forth, and when the strength of the five poisons of sentient beings, the inner **contents**, increases and causes their body, speech and mind to be **full** of non-virtue and **negative** conduct, then, however these **negative conditions** manifest for you, don't accumulate negativity by apportioning blame.

For example, although Jetsun Milarepa and his mother had immeasurable suffering inflicted on them by their close relatives, from these events arose the auspicious conditions for the attainment of buddhahood in one lifetime. Therefore, whatever misfortunes befall you, it is essential to **transform** them **into the path of enlightenment**.

Relative bodhichitta: the method for pacifying all physical and mental suffering

Drive all blame into one.

Whatever happens to you or those close to you, whether a physical malady, mental suffering, gossip, reprimands, lawsuits, robberies or beatings, even if you think it has happened due to the actions of visible enemies or invisible beings such as *dons* and *geks*, or even *mo* divination or astrology, do not blame these.

This ignorant mind grasping at a self within the continuum of mind gives rise to a division of beings between self and other, and upon this basis there amass the variety of non-virtuous actions. This alone, as surely as taking poison results in death, yokes us to suffering in beginningless samsara. Reflect on this, and **drive all blame** onto **one** thing alone: this destructive clinging to self.

Tame ego-clinging through scripture and reasoning. Study and reflect on the words of the Buddha and the commentaries – the manifestations of enlightened speech – and maintain faith and conviction in your heart in the teachings. Shantideva says:

> If all harms in the world, whatever they are,
> And fears and sufferings, as great as there are,
> Come into being by grasping at a self,
> Then what use is this great demon to me?

Furthermore, call on the objects of refuge, the lama and Three Jewels, for aid, and endeavour in supplicating them to grant the realisation of the basic state of non-self.

In summary, having awakened into the Mahayana family and generated the mind of supreme enlightenment, rely on skilful means to attain unsurpassable awakening. The exchange of self and other in thought and action is the essence of the path, and it is important to apply it as well as you can in all situations.

Consider the manner in which the Buddha first produced the mind of supreme enlightenment. While still an ordinary being, he took the agony afflicting the head of another upon himself, and in dependence upon the tiny seed of compassion thus engendered in his heart, meditated throughout many lifetimes until the attainment of buddhahood. Then, turning the wheel of the holy dharma, he dispelled the suffering of numerous sentient beings to be tamed and guided them along the path of liberation.

Also consider that, among all the activities of Milarepa and others, it was through equalizing and exchanging self and other that they attained the final fulfilment of the bodhisattva conduct. However, it would not be correct to 'exchange self and other' by, for example, deliberately setting out to catch an infectious disease. Preoccupied with the miseries of coughing, sneezing and so on, one would be of no use to others whatsoever.

Nevertheless, if it is possible to take another person's sickness, this should be done, in the same way as Gyalse Thogme swapped his good woollen garments for a beggar's lice-infested rags, and wore them without revulsion. If the power of compassion of the Sage is present, as it was in Gyalse Thogme, Guru Maitriyogin, and Jetsun Mila when he accepted poison, this is the right way to practise. However, since we are still enslaved by attachment and self-interest, it is very difficult for us to do this.

Therefore, make aspiration prayers to come to possess this ability in this and all future lifetimes, practise sending and taking which mounts the horse of the breath and, having during this Good Aeon encountered the Vajrayana, which takes the fruit as the path, train in the purification of the vessel and its contents through the emanation and absorption of light by means of the path of the two stages.

Give medicine, food, clothing, and material assistance to those who are enduring physical suffering, and carefully use your resources to benefit those undergoing mental suffering. Take responsibility for anyone who is troubled in body, speech or mind, and train in the bodhisattva conduct of exchanging self and other. Be diligent in skilful means to transform whatever happens into the path of enlightenment.

Reflect on the great kindness of all.

Since the temporary and ultimate benefits of all excellent factors without exception - bodhichitta, the path of application, the six perfections, the four immeasurables and the ultimate level of perfect buddhahood - arise in dependence upon sentient beings, one should **reflect** without partiality **upon the great kindness** of **all**.

Any being that does us harm, whether an enemy, demon or karmic creditor, is a kind friend of the perfection of patience. Pacify any feeling of ill-will towards them, and focus on purifying all the karma, defilements, misdeeds and obscurations that exist within your own mind stream.

By thinking like this, illness in body, suffering in mind, ingratitude for kindness, deceitful friends - in short, anything unwelcome - becomes a broom for our karma and defilements, and exposes the hidden faults of samsara. Thus, that which might previously have discouraged virtue is re-channelled by sending and taking into a virtuous course, and carelessness is put aside.

Using your body, voice and mind, give food, clothing and other necessities, and strive to bring about the welfare and happiness of others. At the same time, recall the great kindness of all sentient beings, both exalted and ordinary, and return that by practising sending and taking. For all beings, including those to whom one is indifferent, follow the words of Shantideva:

Equalize self and others, and
Hold others dearer than yourself.

Continuing to train like this in the meditation of the exchange of self and other, offer direct assistance as much as possible. Help indirectly by training the mind through aspiration and application, and pray for all who are connected to one by positive or negative karma to attain enlightenment.

Persevere in this way in the methods that rely on relative bodhichitta for pacifying all physical and mental suffering.

Ultimate bodhichitta: the method to cut through suffering within the state of emptiness

> **View delusory appearances as the four kayas. The protection of emptiness is unsurpassed.**

Whatever kind of physical or mental suffering arises, establish certainty in the dream-like nature of all internal and external phenomena, which are never experienced as real except as **appearances** created by the power of **deluded** mind.

By looking into mind, the agent of confusion, these **four** are ascertained. The empty essence of mind itself is the dharma**kaya**, its intrinsic luminosity is the immaterial sambhogakaya, the various appearances of samsara and nirvana are the nirmanakaya, and the non-differentiation of these three within naturally existent primordial space[8] constitutes the svabhavikakaya. To settle without distraction within the sphere **of** this **view** is the **protection** of the profound unelaborated **emptiness**.

This is the **unsurpassed** method by which to liberate the illusory appearances of suffering into the expanse of the four buddha kayas. It is important to practise this every day, together with the following.

---

8 Skt. dhatu

The four practices are the supreme method.

The **practices** are gathering the accumulations, confessing negative deeds, offering torma to gods and demons, and offering torma to the dharma protectors. These **four** are the **supreme methods** by which to swiftly pacify all hostile conditions on the path to enlightenment, and to obtain experiential realisation.

1. Gathering the accumulations

Tilopa said:

> Naropa, my son, until you realise
> These dependently arising appearances
> In truth were never born, never part from
> The wheels of your chariot: the two accumulations.

In order to perfect the conceptual accumulation, of merit, protect the vows and pledges of the three vehicles as much as you can. In regard to these excellent precepts, it is said that a good dharma practitioner does not stray from faith and devotion towards even the least part of the training, revering each in the manner of a wish-fulfilling gem raised aloft.

Accordingly, make new representations of the enlightened body, speech and mind, and repair the old ones. Using these as a support, make prostrations and offerings, and pay reverence to the lama and the Three Jewels by reciting the *Seven Branch Prayer*. Provide for the poor and destitute, dispense medicine to the sick, build hospitals, and so on. In short, gather the accumulations to the best of your ability, and make dedications and vast aspiration prayers.

All followers of Tibetan Buddhism take the vows of individual liberation according to their individual circumstances (as a lay follower and so on), the bodhisattva vow, and at least one major empowerment and permission initiation of secret mantra. This is the general situation, which means that it is not only left to the monastic sangha to practise the guarding of conduct. The entire lay and ordained sangha practises acceptance and rejection of virtue and non-virtue, endeavours in skilful means to perfect the great accumulations, and makes aspiration prayers for the name and meaning of 'dharma practitioner' and 'religious country' to become a reality.

Regarding the non-conceptual accumulation, of primordial wisdom, whether we practise the visualisations of mind training or the yogas of the two stages, it is necessary to engage with energy and diligence. Generate the altruistic mind in the preliminary stage, seal any virtue gathered in the main part by the non-objectification of the three circles, and conclude by dedicating the merit. By these 'three holy things', any merit from the practice is added to the sum of the two accumulations.

In particular, settle within the state without grasping, the natural luminous-empty ground of mind itself. This is the way to perfect the great accumulation of ultimate bodhichitta, the seed of the fruit of the dharmakaya.

2. Confession of sins

Due to the power of confused ignorance grasping at a self from time without beginning, we have accumulated a great number of non-virtuous actions. On the basis of the body, these are the ten non-virtues performed through the three gates of body, speech and mind. In particular, they are the breakages of the outer vinaya, of the training of inner Mahayana, and of the pledges of the secret Vajrayana.

Whether or not we are aware of breaking these vows, the power of great laziness, unconcern, the many and forceful defilements and forgetfulness cause faults and downfalls to pour down like a great rain upon dharma bears[9] such as ourselves. For this reason there are the four powers of confession, which are:

- The power of support – the refuge objects
- The power of regret – confession of faults
- The power of antidote – virtuous actions
- The power of resolution – to desist from now on.

By the repeated application of the purifying agent of confession, always in reliance on these four powers, together with prayers such as the threefold recitation of the *Bodhisattva's Confession of Downfalls,* or one hundred repetitions of the hundred-syllable mantra of Vajrasattva, obscurations will swiftly clear. This is called 'the perfection of the great accumulation'.

3. Giving torma to gods and demons

Jetsun Milarepa says:

> As long as mind is ignorant of the all-ground
> The demon of concepts is never exhausted.

Similarly, all the appearances of gods and demons helping or harming us are merely reflections of the ignorance of self-grasping, the deceiving aspect of unborn mind. Nonetheless, until the collapsing of dualistic thought, it is certain that gods and demons will continue to appear to aid and obstruct us. Do not act with aggression towards them, but instead make smoke, torma, and burnt food offerings to them.

In particular, Milarepa says:

> Whoever can offer the skandhas as food
> Knows the path of taming self-clinging.

'To offer the skandhas as food' means to transform one's body into any repast that is desired and to give it away in

9 an incorrigible practitioner; a vow breaker

the 'offering of the body'. It also indicates the practice of compassion through sending and taking.

In summary, make efforts to gladden and placate the gods and demons. In particular, the deities of the dark directions, maras, obstructing spirits and malign spirits were reborn in these forms due to their previous bad actions, and are thus driven to harm others. Therefore, dedicate merit to them, and pray for their negative deeds and obscurations to be completely pacified and that they attain supreme enlightenment.

4. Offering torma to the dharma protectors

The Lord of Sages, the lord of conquerors Padmakara, Zhepa Dorje, and other sublime beings who appeared in the past bound the dharma protectors, along with their consorts and retinues, under oath in order to protect the doctrine and to establish enlightened activities.

Therefore make torma offerings to the protectors, and request them to fulfil their promises. In particular, request those protectors who possess the eye of primordial wisdom to grant the ability to perfect mind training meditation, and to realise non-self, in order to become a source of enlightened activity for the benefit of beings.

'Why are they enjoined to the activity of liberating enemies and obstructors by wrathful means?' It should be understood like this. The dharmapalas employ apparently wrathful acts in order to transfer the consciousness of whomever is to be liberated to Great Bliss, and to prevent them from the further accumulation of negative karma. Since for this it is necessary to hold the compassionate skilful means to be able to lead beings to the level of a buddha in a single instant, it cannot be understood as slaying out of aggression. Thus, through bodhichitta, it never contradicts the mind training. If a competent yogin of secret mantra does not lead the 'ten objects' to liberation, it is said to give rise to a root downfall.

This completes the main part of the present section, 'bringing negative conditions onto the path'.

The Subsequent Stage: To Join Anything That Occurs, Good or Bad, with Meditation Between Sessions

Whatever you meet with now, join it with meditation.

Whatever adverse circumstances you **meet with now** – if you or your friends are subjected to physical or verbal attack, or injury, theft, slander, sudden sickness, reminders of past quarrels and wrongs occur, or if your mind is severely afflicted by the fierce creations of any of the five poisons – bad signs in dreams, visions of spirits and demons, and so on – do not respond to this suffering and ill will by acting from anger, but rely on the compassion of the lama and the Three Jewels. **Meditate** on patience and so forth, and decisively transform whatever you meet into the path of virtue.

These must also be understood as the consequences of countless similar harms we have committed towards others, which have accumulated and are returning to us. Whatever is the case, think, 'May all obstacles and difficulties affecting all sentient beings throughout space be gathered into my own; may they all enjoy happiness and prosperity', and so on. By this, ensure that it becomes second nature to **join** temporary negativity with mind training meditation, and practise sending and taking.

Again, as soon as you experience a little mental ease or enjoyment, the passing pleasures of food, clothing and medicine, the supports of the body, expressions of praise, receiving respect or material gifts, flower gardens, entertainments and dances for the eyes, songs with delightful string accompaniment for the ears, gorgeous aromas for the nose – in short, whatever transient positive factors you meet with at any place or time that bring delight to the heart and mind, think of it as the blessing of the lama and the Three Jewels, and mentally offer a mandala back to them.

Commit to avoiding any increase in self-cherishing due to pride and attachment that may arise from these. Starting with the positive factors you are experiencing now, give all of your happiness, well-being and prosperity to the sentient beings of the six realms, who are poor in joy or pleasure. Combine this with sending and taking.

In summary, Langri Thangpa says:

> The goal of the transformation of adverse conditions into the path of enlightenment is the cessation of hope and fear. For as long as you are unable to bring negative conditions onto the path, these two will not cease. The purifications of tonglen and so on are said to be like straightening a crooked stick.

Moreover, it is of no benefit to boast of a little progress after practising for just a few weeks or months. The practice is said to be for a lifetime.

Point Four

Showing How to Implement the Practice for a Whole Lifetime

The summary of the essence of the pith instructions is this: apply oneself in the five forces.

This **summary of the essence of the pith instructions** condenses the key points of the whole of the holy dharma taught by the Buddha. Therefore it is essential to **adopt the practice** of these **five forces**.

1. The force of resolution

These profound oral instructions of the bodhichitta of mind training are the gateway to the benefit of others, and the remedy that pacifies self-clinging. Do not part from the resolution expressed in the thought: 'From now until the end of this life, I will join whatever I encounter with the practice.'

2. The force of familiarisation

With similar application, wherever you go, whoever you are with, whether you are happy or unhappy, do not be influenced by negative situations, non-virtuous companions, and so forth. Become as familiar as possible with the essential meaning of mind training, the profound view of dependent origination, the supreme meditation of bodhichitta, and the sublime practice of the six perfections. Since their objective is the unsurpassable fruit of buddhahood, pray to the lama and the Three Jewels for harmonious conditions for realisation to arise.

3. The force of virtuous seeds

Once bodhichitta has arisen, to ensure it is not damaged and continually increases, create virtuous seeds through body speech and mind, and engage in skilful means to perfect the two accumulations. Do not neglect even small acts of virtue, such as giving a handful of food to an animal.

4. The force of repudiation

If you contemplate giving up on the benefit of even a single sentient being, or of obtaining advantage from the good you have done, this is to relinquish the bodhisattva aspiration, the jewel of unchanging happiness. If you think like this, repudiate it with intense regret.

5. The force of aspiration

Make aspiration prayers, both in the presence of holy objects or at other times:

> **In general, may I guide all sentient beings to the state of buddhahood. In particular, from now until enlightenment may I never forget the two aspects of the precious bodhichitta even in dreams. May these always increase, and may all difficult situations be transformed into strong friends of bodhichitta.**

Other than this, diligently recite the *King of Aspiration Prayers* and other aspiration prayers of the bodhisattvas from the vast collections in the sutras.

Instructions for the time of death

The essential point of the Mahayana phowa is the five forces. Your conduct is important.

For meditators on mind training, the essence of the **Mahayana**, the profound **essential points of phowa** for the time of death **are** gathered in **the five forces.**

1. The force of virtuous seeds

When a practitioner of mind training arrives at their final illness, they should use whatever great or small wealth they have at their disposal to make offerings and distribute gifts. Having created roots of virtue by giving away without attachment whatever you yourself would wish for, confess all impairments of your vows and pledges.

2. The force of aspiration

> May the sensations, tastes, odours and sweat of the body dissolve and transform into the support and supported of the pure realm of the environment and beings. May my emanations beyond number and measure go forth from there in a single instant and clear away the suffering and causes of suffering of all sentient beings without a single exception. Having placed them in an abundance of happiness together with the causes of happiness, may they enjoy temporary benefits until the attainment of the ultimate state, and be established all at once on the level of buddhahood.

Recite this and other such sublime aspiration prayers.

3. The force of repudiation

Think as follows:

> This ignorant mind of self-grasping has led me through innumerable sufferings of birth, ageing, sickness, and death. Yet although I have experienced these from

> time without beginning, in ultimate truth they are like a dream, not established as truly existent. The all-ground (alaya) and dharmakaya is free of the concept of death. 'Now I am sick; now I am dying' – any thought or feeling such as these is a reflection of self-grasping, and should be let go of.

Aim to become certain of this.

4. The force of resolution

As in the preliminaries, visualise the root lama as the noble supreme Chenrezig at the crown of your head. Make supplications to him and mix your mind with his. Think:

> In the bardo and throughout all my future lives, may I never be separate from the faith of complete reliance on the lama and the Three Jewels, nor from the two aspects of bodhichitta.

Develop this aspiration as much as you can.

5. The force of familiarisation

Whatever strong emotions arise at the time of death, such as aversion to the pain of illness or attachment to friends and relatives, do not become distracted by these. Previously, you meditated on loving-kindness, compassion and the two aspects of bodhichitta. Now, renew these meditations with increased clarity, and focus on sending and taking. Think:

> The true nature of mind, unrecognised up until now, is the authentic ultimate meaning. In the buddha nature itself, birth and death do not exist.

Compose one's mind in meditative equipoise.

At the time of death keep these five forces in mind. At that time, it **is important** to engage in the correct **conduct**. Lie on your right side, your cheek supported by your right hand and so on, in the posture of the 'sleeping Buddha'. The detailed explanations of this may be found elsewhere.

Point Five

The Measure of Mind Training

In the preceding sections the methods to perfect mind training practice have been taught. This section demonstrates how to measure one's progress in this.

The intent of all teachings converges on a single point.

The Blessed One's **intent** in **all** of his enlightened activity, the turning of the vast and profound wheel of the holy **dharma** - the outer pratimoksha, the inner bodhichitta, the secret Mantrayana, and so forth - was nothing other than to tame the unawareness of self-grasping, the root of all faults that lie within the stream of mind. Having understood that all teachings **converge upon** this **single point**, proceed to tame your own mental continuum.

One sign of proficiency in mind training is an increase in the strength of loving-kindness and compassion. This is said to be like a scale weighing the degree to which dharma practice has benefitted the mind.

Of the two witnesses, take the principal one.

There are **two witnesses** to whether you may be described as a good practitioner or not: oneself and others. Since our own mind is not hidden from us, we must **take** the first of these as **the principal one**.

> Others might praise me as a fine practitioner,
> even if it were more fitting to revile me as a base person.

As well as adding to your pride, praise does not benefit the mind, and by rejecting criticism out of hand you will be unable to transform negativity. Therefore, always leave yourself naturally as the witness. If there are no faults to regret, it is a sign of proficiency in the training.

> **Always rely on a joyful mind.**

If you can bring any sufferings and unwanted conditions affecting the body and mind onto the path, this is like adding fuel to a fire. Through the cultivation of the two bodhichittas, they will become friends that will assist you. Therefore **always**, day and night, cultivate mind training as your path of conduct with **a joyful mind**. The ability to **rely** upon this is a sign of proficiency.

> **If you can practise amidst distraction, you are trained.**

Having trained again and again, for a long time, in the words and meaning of mind training texts such as the *Seven Points*, one measure of familiarity is that, due to mindfulness, the mind is not caught up by **distractions** and you recollect the meaning right away. Another is that, even if death arrives without warning, you recollect the auspicious goal of the practice of the two bodhichittas, and do not fear it.

In brief, if the remedies of relative and ultimate bodhichitta are not overwhelmed by any strong negativities that you encounter, and you **can** overcome these right away, this **is** a very wonderful sign of **proficiency**. However, it is of no benefit by itself; it is necessary to perfect this familiarisation by continuing to meditate until the attainment of complete buddhahood.

In summary, if by meditating on sending and taking together you are pervaded by joy, and there is no decline in happiness whatever physical or mental sufferings arise, it is said to be a measure of mastery or proficiency.

Concerning this subject, another Kadampa master stated the following:

> The measure of this training is in turning away;
> The signs of this training are the five greats.

These two lines are explained as follows. The measures of the strong cultivation of altruism are, having turned away with revulsion from holding self dear, to offer gain and victory to others, and the possession of the qualities of the 'five great ones' which follow.

Whoever takes delight in the Mahayana doctrine, trains with faith, and makes bodhichitta the heart of their practice, is a great-minded or heroic being.

Whoever scrupulously avoids the four defeats of an ordained monk or nun, any breakages of the additional vows, and all gross and subtle infringements, and maintains the lineages of non-separation from the correct conduct concerning dharma robes, alms bowl and so on, and the restoration rituals of the new and full moon, and who adheres correctly to the vinaya rules concerning meat, alcohol and eating after midday, is a great abbot, a holder of the vinaya.

Whoever has the ability to overcome the defilements by the practice of austerities is a great ascetic.

Whoever remains inseparable from the ten spiritual activities is a great mendicant.

Whoever remains inseparable from the experiential state of emptiness and compassion is a great yogin.

To attain these five, it is said to be essential to keep the precepts, even when the right way to practise becomes difficult to guard due to the influence of impure times, places and companions.

Point Six

Pledges of Mind Training

The sixteen pledges to be guarded by mind training practitioners are as follows.

1. Always train in the three general points.

Having gone for refuge to the Three Jewels, study the path of the three trainings. These being the **points** held in **general**, a mind training practitioner will also maintain the following:

I. The mind training of not breaking pledges.

II. The mind training of not straying into foolish conduct.

III. The mind training of not straying into partiality.

You must **always train in these three.**

I. Whichever major or minor precepts of the three vehicles you have promised to uphold, strive to avoid the taint of moral faults with mindfulness, clear comprehension and concern. If a fault occurs, aim to purify it right away by confession.

II. Do not act impulsively to show off your lack of ego-clinging, by covering your home or shrine with dust or ash, eating spoiled food, dressing shabbily, and so on. Don't engage in senseless conduct such as sleeping in wild places, cutting down special trees, destroying sacred objects or travelling to the locality of epidemics. Instead, follow the examples of outer and inner purity according to the tradition of Geshe Dromtonpa and the biographies of the holy Kadampas. These yogins of mind training meditation possessed immaculate purity in body and mind and were a source of happiness wherever they went.

III. Renounce partiality, such as working for the benefit of some beings but not for others, offering respect to high status individuals while showing contempt for low, practising mind training towards sentient beings but not in regard to the elements, or having patience with friends and relatives but not with enemies. It is essential not to fall into one-sidedness.

2. Change your attitude while remaining natural.

Change the motivation you have held until now, that of cherishing self over others, by seizing hold of the care of others. Be insatiable in the practice of the outer dharma, and resolve to **keep your** conduct **natural**, in harmony with all beings good or bad.

Inwardly, become very familiar with the practice. Do not separate even for a moment from the practices of bodhichitta, such as the exchange of self and other. In this way, like the swiftest of horses, you will traverse a vast expanse of ground.

3. Do not talk about weak points.

Whether out of jealousy or bad character, at **no** time, even at the cost of your life, call out about others' **weak**nesses of mobility or posture, learning disability and so on, whether they are male or female, young or old. Likewise do not **talk** judgmentally about weaknesses in another's dharma practice, such as inconsistency, loss of monastic vows, fondness for donations, hypocrisy, deception, and so forth.

It is not appropriate even to despise yourself. You have the freedoms and endowments, the bases of liberation, and the complete mandalas of the 'deities of the three seats' are present, as it is said.

4. Do not dwell on the faults of others.

As well as discarding outward negative words and looks, **do not dwell** inwardly **on whatever faults there are in others**. If you should see or hear of some defect, compare it to your own heap of faults. Instead of dwelling on whatever faults others might have, think about the benefits of mind training, of putting others before yourself and so on, and use its methods to reverse the flaws within your own character.

In particular, do not conceive of the presence of faults in your root lamas. Through an old woman's pure vision, even the tooth of a dog was transformed into a sacred relic. By contrast, the inconstant view of impure vision, when faith and gratitude are forgotten, resembles that of Devadatta, the monk Sunakshatra, and a certain tirthika who saw faults even in the Buddha. Therefore, dispel doubt and wrong views from your mind.

According to the sutras and tantras, it is rare in a dark age to find a spiritual master with the authentic characteristics. Whether your lama really does possess faults or not, by maintaining pure vision towards him or her, the jewel of your pledges will naturally be cleansed.

5. Purify the strongest defilement first.

Due to attachment and aversion, I am devoted exclusively to my own interests, while those who are not like me will not fail to move forward on the spiritual path, and their minds will not be harsh and uneven like a briar patch, or constantly busy like a monkey.

Thus, **purify** whichever **defilement** is **strongest** in your mind stream **first**, such as attachment to the respect of friends and neighbours, or jealousy of those who receive this. Do this purification by heaping all of the antidotes upon it. Similarly, learn from the first to let go of bad companions, who are poor examples of virtue and who increase the defilements.

6. Give up all hope of results.

Whether making offerings to holy beings or giving help and support to the poor and destitute – in short, whatever great or small roots of virtue you engage in – **give up all expectation** of self-serving **results** such as fame or reputation.

7. Give up poisoned food.

Eating **food** mixed **with poison** results in death. Likewise, virtue motivated by the defilements, such as ignorance that conceives of a truly existent self and truly existent external objects, does not lead to liberation but binds us in samsara.

Since this result is suffering, fully implement the antidotes such as the 'three holy things', and learn to abandon that which is to be rejected. Furthermore, **give up** dissolute lifestyles, and food and drink that make you vulnerable to illness.

8. Do not pretend to a good nature.

To outwardly **pretend to a good nature** while harbouring malicious thoughts that spring from a negative inward disposition, clinging to old grievances in your heart, fixating on arguments and so on, is a way of living harmful to mind training. Reject it. Furthermore, do not put on a front to impress non-virtuous friends. The way others behave towards us will always fluctuate, so **do not** depend on them in your heart.

9. Don't make malicious jokes.

A mind training meditator will **not** hide behind humour as a pretext to make **malicious jokes** that expose the hidden flaws of others. Abandon the tendency towards cruelty.

10. Don't wait in ambush.

If you **never** forget some injustice done to you or your friends, harbouring that resentment in your heart even after many years, it is like **waiting** by a narrow pass in order to **ambush** and dispatch an enemy. Don't match harm for harm, either by using harsh words, or physically by throwing stones and so on. From lifetimes without beginning, the true enemy has been our inner self-grasping. Therefore, using patience and the sword of profound emptiness, strike at the neck of your own rancour and aggression.

11. Don't strike at the vital point.

Refrain from evil actions harmful to another's body, life or good fortune. Do not seek to shame and ruin a rival with false accusations, and do not use black magic or evil mantras to steal the life force of humans or non-humans. **Do not strike at vital points** to cause harm, either physically or mentally.

12. Don't burden an ox with the load of a dzo.

To lay the burden of an arduous task that is intended for you onto someone else is like over-**burdening** an **ox** with a heavy **load** meant for a **dzo**. **Do not** do this. Likewise, don't try to lay the blame for faults such as lying, theft, or even the breakage of household wares, onto subordinates and suchlike.

13. Don't sprint to win a race.

If you attempt to obtain the greater share of food and gifts from among many people, you are like a rider **sprinting** for the finish in a horse **race**, and will feel anger and resentment if you fail to carry off the prize. Therefore, wherever there is disagreement about common funds, property, donations and so on, **do not** behave as if you were trying to **win** a race.

14. Don't poison your food.

Even if you practise the holy dharma, mind training and so on, if it is reduced to a mere method to accomplish the eight worldly dharmas, the concerns of this life, it will be lost. This would be like eating a spoiled meal. Since it would then be necessary to purge such **poisoned food** by vomiting it up, **avoid** this.

15. Do not lower a deity to a demon.

If you practise mind training but your mind becomes more harsh, and you look down upon and disparage others, thinking that you are better than them and so on, all the training will be lost.

Moreover, if you perform wrathful rituals to invoke those such as the dharma protectors in order to, for example, crush an enemy who has harmed a relative or friend, even if the **deity** is a wisdom being, it is effectively **lowered to a demon** because your motivation has descended into aggression. **Do not** alter it in this manner.

16. Do not pursue misery as a condition of happiness.

Thoughts such as 'If my rivals are gone, I will enjoy success and honour', 'It does not matter if others are unhappy, as long as my loved ones and I prosper', and 'If I gain a reputation as a good dharma practitioner, I will obtain food, wealth and renown' all represent attitudes and conduct inimical to mind training. If you cultivate your own **happiness** in particular, this will make it **conditional** on **misery**. Therefore **never look** for it in this way; it is incorrect to do so, as it is said.

Treat these sixteen pledges in the same way as the essence vows of the paths of other vehicles. Guard them with mindfulness, clear comprehension and concern, without infringing them in a single detail. If you or anyone else do break their commitments, treat your own breakages as the chief among these, and sincerely confess to the non-virtuous actions and errors in thought and conduct of all sentient beings.

Point Seven

Precepts of Mind Training

The following twenty-two precepts show what is to be accepted and what is to be rejected, and will be of benefit for the lifelong practice of the profound mind training of equalizing and exchanging self and other, the essence of the Mahayana.

1. Practise all yogas as one.

While other systems of practice treat the yogas of eating, sleeping and so forth as separate, this is not necessary in mind training. It is sufficient to **practise** just **one yoga** at all times: never to forget the training. Whatever you are doing, **al**ways think about how you can help others.

It is also possible to integrate the yogas of everyday life, such as eating and sleeping, into this practice. By adherence to the *Mind Training of the Eight Sessions*, realisation will be attained.

2. Use the same solution for everything.

If, while practising the teachings, great obstacles and adversity arise, such as frequent sickness, malicious rumours, loss of friends and appropriate conditions, the intensification of disturbing emotions, or weariness with the dharma, and from this there comes doubt, discouragement and loss of interest in doing virtue through body, speech and mind, think as follows:

> There are many beings in this world, such as myself, who do not act in accord with the holy dharma. I take all of the negative conceptualizations of all sentient beings for myself, and give all of my body, wealth, and virtue to them. Through this, may they enter the path of unmistaken thought and conduct.

Among **all** remedies to hindrances, this is the best of **solutions**. Also, pledge to abandon apathy and doubt regarding the dharma. By **single**-mindedly **practising** sending and taking for the benefit of others, you will have done enough. You may also read of the immense qualities and benefits of meditation on bodhichitta in the sutras and shastras.

3. At the beginning and the end do two things.

If you are a layman or laywoman, when you get up in the morning, make the resolution that today you will avoid whatever is contrary to the holy dharma, such as arguing, striking or killing vulnerable beings, taking beer, spirits, or tobacco, swearing, oath-making or using confusing or misleading speech.

If you are ordained, think that today, with mindfulness, clear comprehension and concern for the training, you will avoid engaging in negative thoughts and actions towards other beings, actions based on self-clinging, but instead cherish them tirelessly.

Make this recollection early in the morning whenever possible, and upon this basis make efforts in skilful means. In either case, this very day, at this very hour, take hold of your bodhisattva vows. Generate this altruistic intention at the commencement of any activity, and then rely upon mindfulness.

At the end of your final session of meditation, or just before you fall asleep, examine your mental continuum for positive or negative actions performed during the day. Confess anything against the Mahayana doctrine and dedicate any merit to the welfare of others. Thus strive to **do** these **two things**: to enumerate virtue and non-virtue **at** both **the beginning and the end** of the day.

4. Whichever of the two occurs, have patience.

We may enjoy the happiness of security and plentiful **provisions, but** if we are unserious and of little sense, we may fail to use this as a support for our practice. If this happens, we will lose concern for religious conduct, such as the keeping of vows and pledges, and thus abandon it. Likewise, if our body and mind are continually afflicted by many sufferings, we will not be able to bear them, and then abandon the dharma. Consequently, **whichever of the two occurs**, joy or sorrow, they will act as an obstacle rather than a support.

So do not be absorbed by either of these. Happiness may be the fruit of tiny merits from former lives, or the blessing of the lama and the Three Jewels. Suffering may be the result of our past negative deeds in samsara, or obstacles created by malign forces.

Whatever the case may be, determine to respond to injury with loving-kindness and compassion, and, whether happiness or misery arise, equalize them as one taste. In summary, it is said that those noble ones of gentle nature who are engaged in the excellent conduct of the bodhisattvas must rely upon the armour of **patience**.

5. Protect the two, even if your life is threatened.

The general pledges of the holy dharma consist of the abandonment of harm and the basis of harm to others, and the adoption of the benefit and basis of the benefit of others, while the special pledges of mind training are those taught here. If either of **these two** pledges declines, they will not be a source of happiness in this and future lives.

In particular, they will not act as a suitable foundation for the path of meditation on the bodhichitta of the exchange of self and other. For this reason, they must be **protected even if your life is threatened**. For example, even if someone were to hold a knife to your heart and say, 'Abandon the Three Jewels and the mind of enlightenment, or I will kill you', you do not give them up.

6. Train in the three difficult things.

Due of the power of our familiarity with the defilements, at the very moment that any of the five poisons are first produced, to us it is as if they had already arisen. Therefore, to recognise them in that moment is difficult. Then, when conditions gather to produce aggression and so forth, it is difficult to curb them immediately with the antidotes such as loving-kindness. Finally, it is **difficult** to cut the continuity of the defilements to prevent them from arising again.

Even before a defilement such as hatred is first produced, ensure that you are guarded by mindfulness. Remain within this without distraction. By the force of full application, you will develop the ability to become aware of the defilements at the very point of their arising. **Train** like this, to avoid being subject to the power of these **three things**.

7. Cultivate the three principal causes.

The three principal causes of genuine dharma practice are:

- The qualified lama who is the guide to the path
- The joyful wish to put the teachings into practice
- The possession of favourable conditions such as ease of obtaining food and clothing.

Since these are essential, be joyful when they are assembled for you, and rejoice in their gathering for others. By **cultivating** them now, they will become easier to find in the future. Furthermore, when we enjoy such prosperity ourselves, we should help to bring about similar conditions for other practitioners.

8. Unfailingly cultivate the three things.

These are:

- Unfailing devotion towards the lama, the guide to bodhichitta
- Unfailing faith and energy in meditation on the bodhichitta of the exchange of self and other, which leaves discouragement and considerations of difficulty far behind, however many months or years pass
- **Unfailing** acceptance and rejection, never forgetting the pledges and precepts of mind training.

With mindfulness, clear comprehension and concern, be inseparable from the **cultivation** and application of these **three things**. If faith and devotion towards the lama declines, the door to the development of qualities will close. If faith, devotion and joyful enthusiasm for the practice deteriorates, there will be no space for bodhichitta to develop. If concern for the training declines, there will be no ground from which qualities can develop.

9. Possess the three inseparables.

Bringing about as much benefit as you can, become inseparable from virtue practised through the body. Abandon non-virtues of body such as taking life. Do prostrations and circumambulations, make pure offerings and keep the inside and outside of the temple clean. Serve your lamas and parents, and provide medicine, food, clothing and shelter to the sick and impoverished.

As far as possible, become inseparable from virtuous speech, and abandon non-virtuous speech such as lying and slander. Use your speech for prayers and recitations, and practise sending and taking on the breath at least one hundred times a day if possible. Furthermore, explain the dharma, compose texts and so on.

Abandon non-virtues of mind, such as malevolence, and become inseparable from the mental virtues such as renunciation, bodhichitta and the view of emptiness. Always **possess** these **three inseparables**.

10. Don't take sides.

Practise without bias – without the **partiality** of thinking, 'I will meditate for them, but not for *them*'. Take enemies, friends, humans and non-humans alike as **objects** of meditation on loving-kindness, compassion and sending and taking.

11. All training must be deep and pervasive.

Whatever actions you carry out with body, speech or mind, they should be **pervaded** alone by bodhichitta, which is neither mere words **nor** mere mindfulness. You **must al**ways practise the skilful means of the **training** from the very **depths** of your heart.

12. Always meditate on particular cases.

Pay attention to **particular cases**, such as serious harm-doers who strongly perturb your mind, very aggressive visible and invisible enemies, or those who respond to kindness with injury. **Always cultivate** loving kindness and compassion towards these in particular.

Likewise, train to meditate on sentient and insentient entities that make you restless and agitated, whether they swell your pride or act as objects of attachment, as the illusory and insubstantial objects of the three circles, impermanent, compounded phenomena devoid of an innate essence.

13. Don't rely on external conditions.

While the presence of many favourable conditions - a good livelihood, freedom from illness, and so on - are a prerequisite for other spiritual practices such as sadhana recitation in retreat, mind training **does not rely** upon **external factors** in this way. Even the absence of positive conditions and the increase of hindrances can act as the very harmonious conditions favourable to this practice. They are transformed by the bodhichitta of the exchange of self and other.

14. Practise the main point right now.

Although **at present** we possess two goals, a spiritual and a worldly one, now that we have understood the significance of having attained a human body with the freedoms and endowments, we must accomplish the **main point**, the excellent dharma, the object of which is unchanging bliss.

Furthermore, while there are many ways to meditate, as a true cause of buddhahood, bodhichitta is said to be without peer. Its essence is the cultivation of mind training. So just **practise** this. Make it your principal activity above all the other things of this life.

Moreover, as Shantideva says:

There is no negativity like anger
And no austerity like patience.

Among the defilements, the chief deputies of self-clinging are anger and jealousy, bringing us continual destruction in this and future lives. The best way to overcome their force is the assiduous cultivation of patience. This is a key point.

15. Don't be mistaken.

We must abandon six misinterpretations and adhere to six unmistaken understandings.

An individual who has promised to accomplish nothing but the holy dharma in this life – the excellent mind training and so forth – will undertake conduct that is difficult for the sake of this dharma. To lack patience with getting up early, or going to bed a little late for the sake of the dharma, but to do the same in order to engage in any kind of non-virtuous occupation whatsoever, is mistaken patience.

Kharag Gomchung and other venerable Kadampa lamas aspired to the skilful means for the realisation of the pure and excellent doctrine, which is of complete benefit. Not to do this, but to aspire instead to the glory, renown, happiness, comforts and so forth of this life, the eight worldly dharmas, is mistaken aspiration.

Not to relish the taste of exceptional bliss, experienced through meditation on relative and ultimate bodhichitta, but to cling instead to the taste of desired worldly objects such as material wealth, beer, spirits, tobacco and so forth, is mistaken enjoyment.

To lack compassion towards evildoers who have committed the ten non-virtues, who wage world war and so on, while fostering compassion towards those who practise austerities for the sake of the dharma, who endure hardships to guard their vows, and keep the three, food, clothing and chatter, to a bare minimum, is mistaken compassion.

To refrain from wholesome conduct in harmony with the dharma, such as modesty at friendly gatherings, but instead to become involved in negative worldly activities such as protecting friends and defeating enemies out of partiality, and the trio of dishonesty, pretence and deception, is mistaken engagement.

The Buddha declared that any great or small happiness enjoyed by sentient beings is the fruit of corresponding great or small virtue. Since this is so, to reject delighting in virtue while revelling in jealousy and misery is **mistaken** rejoicing.

All harmful errors in conflict with the virtuous actions of the three gates are included in these six. **Avoid** these mistakes.

16. Don't fluctuate.

When I am comfortable, well fed and warmed by the sun, I have the form of a practitioner.
When adversity prevails, I become an ordinary person.

Just like this, despite pledging to devote our lives to the dharma, we only practise when times are good, we have what we need and are respected by others. If we stop practising when these are absent, this is a sign that definitive knowledge is yet to arise in our heart. **Do not fluctuate** in this way. Whether things go well or badly, sustain your efforts like an ever-flowing river.

17. Practise with focus.

Throughout all your activities, whether in motion or at rest, don't allow yourself to be affected by distractions, idle chatter, and so forth. Just **focus** on bodhichitta and **practise** with one-pointed determination.

18. Liberate yourself through both reflection and analysis.

Always **reflect** on your body, speech and mind, and use **analysis** to examine whether your deeds are virtuous or non-virtuous. Apply **both** of these carefully, until they become second nature. If you reach a point where you think you are in control of your mind, check whether strong attachment or aversion still arises in conditions similar to before. If they do, apply all the antidotes again straight away. It is vital to **liberate yourself** from such negativity, as it is said.

19. Don't boast.

Whether you are ordained, or a lay man or woman, although you may have made steps in purifying the obscurations, gathering the accumulations and so on, and performed excellent deeds through body, speech and mind for the benefit of others, it is also excellent to **discard** the habit of **boasting** of these to others. It is you who are the main beneficiary of having come to possess the qualities needed to be a Mahayana practitioner, of being accepted by a spiritual master, and having received direct instructions in the means to accomplish the dharma.

20. Don't lose control out of irritation.

If an employee, colleague or assistant makes a minor error in trivial conflict with our preference, as a mind training practitioner we must **not lose control out of** any kind of **irritation** in any of our conduct, for example by reacting with sudden anger, glowering or issuing harsh rebukes. Whatever happens, keep an open heart and act with generosity. Never deviate at any time from a gentle course.

Potawa once said:

> Because we practitioners don't use the dharma as a remedy for self-clinging, we are more sensitive than a newly healed wound, and more irritable than

Tsangtsen. This is not useful dharma. To be useful, the dharma must work as a remedy for self-clinging.

21. Don't be inconstant.

Unless we have a foundation of stability and self-control, we will easily be influenced by positive and negative friends, and if our conduct of body, speech and mind is **inconstant**, we will continue to wander in transmigratory existence. **Do not** act like this.

22. Don't expect thanks.

Just help everyone, whoever they are, as well as you can. When it comes to **thanks**, don't wait to hear expressions of gratitude, such as: 'You are so kind!' Whatever virtue you perform using your body, speech, mind and possessions, don't hanker after praise and adulation. It is taught that mind training practitioners **do not expect** this.

~

This essence of the nectar of the pith instructions
Which transforms the rampant five degenerations
Into the path of enlightenment
Is a transmission from Serlingpa.

In these evil days, the **five impurities** are very powerful and **on the increase**, so it is difficult to bring temporary adverse conditions onto the path by means of other dharmas. However, an individual versed in the profound practice of mind training, the bodhichitta of exchanging self and other, will be able to transform as many undesirable conditions as there are into effective aids to practice. In this way, they can **transform** them **into the path of enlightenment**. This special dharma is not to be found elsewhere. These **pith instructions** of the venerable Kadampas for taming self-clinging are the **essence** of all sections of the dharma, and are like an excellent medicinal **nectar** for curing sickness.

Among the three gurus, it was **Serlingpa** Dharmakirti who introduced the special experiential bodhichitta to Atisha. The **lineage** of this tradition proceeded to Atisha's principal spiritual son Dromtonpa, then to the spiritual master Potawa Rinchen Sal, then to Geshe Sharawa Yonten Drak. Following these four, the injunction of bodhichitta was bestowed on Chekhawa Yeshe Dorje.

> **The awakening of residual karma from former training**
> **Caused my devotion to increase.**
> **So, scorning suffering and criticism from that time forward,**
> **I requested the oral instructions for subduing self-clinging.**
> **Now even in death I'll have no regrets.**

The awakening of residual karma from the great spiritual teacher Chekhawa's **former training caused** his heart's **devotion** to the mind training that subdues self-clinging **to increase**, not just for a short time, but continually thereafter. Thus, to begin with he sought the teachings, then put them into practice at all times, undergoing hardship and **scorning** all **suffering** as well as the **criticisms** and harsh comments of others.

Thus he **requested the oral instructions for subduing self-clinging**, and relied on the training in the proper manner. By the practice of the bodhichitta of holding others dearer than self, he achieved mastery over his mental continuum. **Then**, since he had completely perfected his heart intention, **even** at the time of **death he had no regrets**.

~

This completes the main part of this commentary on the *Seven Points*. However my own powers are measured, these annotations are offered with pure intention.

Additional Instructions from the Lineage

These instructions, appended to the *Direct Path to Enlightenment* and summarized here, are extremely beneficial for eliminating obstacles to mind training meditation.

Anything that a lifelong mind training meditator wishes for, whether a pleasant place to live, a good bed, the respect and service of others, and so on, will be exceeded. Later, bliss, joy and an abundance of desirable things will arise. Should the negative discriminations of a conceited mind arise, stealing away the wealth of contentment which has few desires, respond by targeting satire at oneself.

The great lord Serlingpa said:

With a grasping disposition such as yours,
It is remarkable that you even have this home and bed,
Or that you even remain sane.
By persisting in this way towards others,
It is a great fortune not to be reborn in hell;
It is a great fortune not to be cooked to a cinder.

This means that, if we have become a slave to self-clinging, our basic state of mind being negative and our mind never having mixed with the dharma, it is remarkable that we have even found a place to live and a bed to sleep in.

Furthermore, despite being dominated by the habit of negative conceptualization, we have not been driven insane by the demon of self-clinging. Instead our mind is healthy and resides in its ordinary state.

Not only that, considering our great persistence in behaving non-virtuously, and being unable to bear any difficulty at all in acting well towards others, it is a great fortune not to have been reborn yet again in hell as the fruit of this, and a great fortune not to be experiencing the arrival of the servants of hell in person, and the suffering of being cooked to a cinder.

Thus it is said that one must inculcate a sense of shame in oneself. Serlingpa said:

> **Moreover, strongly contemplating such a dreadful danger,**
> **You should be driven by a great sense of shame.**
> **Live austerely and eat no more than you need.**
> **Accept a low place and dress frugally.**
> **Disregarding happiness and suffering, work on the antidotes.**

This is easy to understand. Concerning the mind training dharma:

> **In solitude it is a comfort.**
> **In illness it is a nurse.**

When anguished by deep sorrow, although the mind is compelled to look to worldly friendship, it is difficult to find the help hoped for. Lama Chagme declared:

> Bodhichitta is the cause of eternal bliss.

Thus, mind training is a consolation at times of solitude, and similarly, when we fear the pain of disease and illness, it is a nurse. Although it is difficult always to find the support we are hoping for, if we become inseparable from the company of the bodhichitta of mind training it will always sustain us, both day and night, like the best nurse. Since the very extensive benefits of immutable happiness will arise, there is no reason to place hope or fervour in other objects.

Serlingpa instructed Atisha: 'In order to tame the barbarian borderlands in this dark age, you must teach the oral instructions.'

Level all thoughts;
Strike with all antidotes to subdue.
Unify all counsels or plans;
All paths converge in one place.
These four dharmas are the purifying agents;
They are needed for taming the borderlands.
For patience with false practices and bad companions,
They are called for in corrupted times.

When conceptualizations based on the defilements and so on are produced, level them immediately. Strike at them straight away with the antidotes that subdue the factors to be abandoned. All paths are unified in the goal of taming self-grasping, and once self-clinging is tamed, this is sufficient for the paths and bhumis. Therefore, all remedies pertaining to complete purification are encapsulated in these four.

Adverse conditions are spiritual friends.
Maras and demons are emanations of the Victorious One.
Illness is a broom that sweeps away sins and obscurations.
Suffering is the display of dharmata.
These four dharmas are the pervading defilements;
They are needed for taming the borderlands.
For patience with false practices and bad companions,
They are called for in corrupted times.

The four phenomena of the pervading defilements are adverse conditions, maras and demons, illness, and suffering. Since these four are spiritual friends, aids to liberation, it is not necessary to abandon them. This is a pointing out instruction.

Happiness greatly suppresses.
Suffering greatly concludes.
Difficulties are greatly treasured.
Bad omens are taken as great wealth.
These four dharmas act as counteragents;
They are needed for taming the borderlands.
For patience with false practices and bad companions,
They are called for in corrupted times.

When physical or mental well-being arises, think that it represents all happiness and joy and send it to beings. Train in the emptiness of the essence of the actual concepts of enjoyment. To conceive of the defilements such as pride and attachment as enjoyment suppresses.

Likewise, when suffering arises, accept the suffering of all sentient beings and add it to your own. Use the taste of this suffering to substitute yourself for all beings, who are sinking in the swamp of suffering. Thinking, 'May they be happy', settle in equanimity in the expanse of emptiness, the actual nature of suffering. This training is the conclusion of suffering.

Similarly, if you become the unwelcome object of gossip, slander or litigation, put aside the error of self-clinging. Since these things can serve to sever us from the great hope and fear that accompany self-cherishing, they are treasured friends to mind training. Bring them onto the path.

Furthermore, negative portents of any kind - serious illnesses, fierce defilements, phantasmal displays of gods and demons, curses, bindings and so on - can act as helpmates and enrich our cultivation of mind training.

These four dharmas act as counter-agents for those untamed by other remedies.

Self is the root of all faults;
This dharma leaves it far away.
Others are the source of qualities;
This dharma accepts them and holds them fast.
These two dharmas summarize the remedies.
They are needed for taming the borderlands.
For patience with false practices and bad companions,
They are called for in corrupted times.

The self is the root of karma and the defilements and the foundation of suffering, therefore let go of clinging to self-cherishing. The source of temporary and ultimate benefit, including the level of buddhahood, is other sentient beings, therefore embrace them. All remedies are included in these two, abandoning and accepting.

Turn error around and look directly in.
Rest at ease and completely relax.
What is not bound will be liberated.

With a mind undistracted by external concerns, turn inwards. Eradicate grasping at artificial modifications and relax freely, without conceptualization, in the clear cognition of the state of the unelaborated dharmadhatu, free of subject and object. Rest in this without fixation. In this way, not bound by samsara, the defilements will be liberated into primordial wisdom.

Arya Maitreya

Conclusion

The Benefits and Qualities of a Lifetime's Endeavour in the Practice of Mind Training

Physical illness, harmful spirits and all negative deeds and obscurations will be exhausted. Obstacles will be transformed into sources of accomplishments, and one will enjoy the affection of gods, spirits and human beings. One's fame will spread in every direction. Acquiring food, wealth, friends and a retinue, one will enjoy happiness in body, facility in speech, while realisation will blaze up in mind. Any sentient being who sees one will receive blessings, their obscurations of karma and the defilements will be purified, and they will ultimately obtain the great enlightenment. Thus it is said that the benefits and qualities are beyond measure.

Furthermore, in Lord Lodro Thaye's extensive commentary it says:

> The root of the sutra and tantra paths,
> Essence nectar of all the holy dharma,
> Profound yet blissful to practice,
> It is a marvel among all modes of teaching.
>
> A profound dharma like this is difficult to hear.
> Being heard, it is difficult to put into practice.

To act on this is to be rich in merit,
As rare these days as gold on the ground.

In accordance with this, even if you only receive the reading transmission and explanation of this profound dharma, good fortune is beyond doubt. Therefore commit yourself to its practice.

~

Although adorned with the beautiful gems of the three vows,
Due to laziness, the thieves of the defilements have risen up.
So, parroting this profound dharma which is like a *maṇi* jewel,
I have arranged these annotations to refresh my memory a little.

By the flowing camphor river of jewel-like good actions,
Dispelling the intense torment of suffering of limitless beings,
May there be the victory for living beings of the holy level
Of the Blessed One, the ultimate vision of appearances.

Because I received the transmission and explanation of the *Direct Path to Enlightenment*, this short annotative commentary on the *Seven Points of Mind Training,* entitled *Dispelling the Darkness of Suffering*, conforms to the root text of that work. Ornamented by the holy words of others, and mainly for the ease of my own understanding and recollection, I have written these lines on the development of the mind of enlightenment.

By the virtue of this composition, completed in the great northern country (Canada) by Karma Thinleypa, one who holds merely the external signs of a follower of Shakya, may the entire world be completely freed from every kind of karmic cause and effect, and from the sufferings of disease, famine, conflict and war, and may every being be united with the most glorious, powerful, and excellent benefits. May the newly risen sun of the mind training instructions, the profound whispered lineage of the venerable Kadampas, blaze forth in every direction.

The Tibetan text was published by Rigdzin Khandro. May virtue increase.

Biography of Karma Thinley Rinpoche

Karma Thinley Rinpoche, master of the Kagyu and Sakya traditions, was born into the noble family of Bongsar in 1931 in the Nangchen area of Kham, Eastern Tibet. At the age of one month, he received refuge and some two years later was recognized by the then head of the Sakya tradition, Sakya Trizin Dagshul Thinley Rinchen, as the tulku (incarnation) of the Sakyapa master Biru Sharyak Lama Kunrik, thought to be an incarnation of the great Vairochana. At that time he received all the symbols and titles of his rank and authority.

Owing to Rinpoche's rank and the extraordinary profusion of spiritual masters among his extensive set of relations, he received a vast number of teachings during his childhood and youth. From his uncle, the famous yogin and terton Jigje Lama, he received various Kagyu and Nyingma precepts, as he did from his two great uncles Shabtrung Rinpoche and Pangchog Rinpoche, heads of Riwoche, the famous non-sectarian monastery. From the great Sakya masters Khangsar Khenpo Ngawang Yonten Gyamtso and Ngawang Tashi Chophel, he received a wide range of Sakyapa teachings.

At such monasteries as Lachung, Dilyak and Neten, Rinpoche studied the classical Mahayana texts under a number of masters, including Khenpo Paddam, Khenpo Gurga, Drupon Sanjay Puntsok and Khenpo Tsegyam. Later at Tsurphu in Central Tibet, Rinpoche received full monastic ordination from H.H. 16th Gyalwa Karmapa. It was during this period that H.H. Karmapa recognized Rinpoche as the fourth incarnation of Karma Thinleypa, the famous Kagyu and Sakya scholar.

In 1959 Rinpoche left Tibet in the party of the Karmapa, fleeing from communist oppression. Subsequently Rinpoche became abbot of a newly established nunnery at Tilokpur in 1962. In 1967 he received The Path and its Fruit, the principal cycle of teachings of the Sakya tradition, from H.H. Sakya Trizin at Sarnath. It was about this time that Rinpoche met his first Western disciples. In 1971 Rinpoche settled in Canada, accompanying a group of Tibetan refugees as their spiritual teacher, and a year later founded the Tibetan Society, to introduce Tibetan culture to Canada. In 1973 Rinpoche founded Kampo Gangra Drubgyud Ling meditation centre in Toronto, named after the first Karmapa's monastery in Kham. That same year Rinpoche spent three months in Scotland, where he met his English student Lama Jampa Thaye for the first time.

Karma Thinley Rinpoche returned to India in 1978 to receive the *Rinchen Terdzod*, the famous collection of Nyingma treasure cycles, from H.H. Dingo Khyentse Rinpoche. Four years later, he made his first return to Tibet for over twenty years, travelling throughout Nangchen visiting his relatives and giving teachings. In 1983 Rinpoche received the *Drubthab Kuntu*, the collected sadhanas of the new tantra schools, from H.E. Chogye Trichen in Lumbini.

Over the last fifty years Rinpoche has founded centres and taught extensively in Canada, the USA, New Zealand and the United Kingdom. He has hundreds of devoted students, both Tibetan and Western. In addition to being an accomplished poet and artist, Rinpoche is a renowned historian, having written (in English) *The History of the Sixteen Karmapas*. His major projects at the current time are the continuing supervision of his nunnery Tegchen Legshay Ling in Boudhanath, Nepal and Sangngak Phodrang in Nangchen.

The Tibetan Text

གཅིག

༄༅། །ཐེག་པ་ཆེན་པོའི་བློ་སྦྱོང་དོན་བདུན་མའི་ཚིག་འགྲེལ་མདོར་བསྡུས་སྡུག་བསྔལ་མུན་སེལ་ཞེས་བྱ་བ་བཞུགས་སོ།།

1

༄༅། །ཨོཾ་སྭ་སྟི། །མཁྱེན་པའི་མཁའ་ལ་ཐུགས་རྗེའི་ཆུ་འཛིན་དཀྲིགས། །རླབས་ཆེན་ཕྲིན་ལས་ནུས་པའི་གྲུ་ཆར་གྱིས། །མཐའ་ཡས་
འགྲོ་ལ་ཕན་བདེའི་པད་ཚལ་བསྐྱེད། །མཉམ་མེད་སྟོན་མཆོག་ཤཱཀྱའི་དབང་པོར་འདུད། །སྨྲུན་སྟོང་ཨུཏྤལ་རྒྱས་པའི་ཟེའུ་འབྲུ་ལས། །ཐུགས་རྗེའི་
ཆུ་རྒྱུན་སུ་ཧྲིག་ཐིགས་འཕྲེང་འཛེ། །འགྲོ་བའི་གདུང་སེལ་བླ་མ་སྤྱན་རས་གཟིགས། །དབྱེར་མེད་ཞབས་སེན་ནོར་བུ་གཙུག་ཏུ་ལེན། ཐེག་ཆེན་བདུད་
རྩིའི་བཅུད་བཟང་བློ་སྦྱོང་ཆོས། །རྒྱལ་བཞིན་སྒོམ་པའི་རང་ནུས་དབེན་ན་ཡང་། །ཚིག་ཙམ་རློམས་ཀྱང་སླལ་པ་སྒོམ་པའི་ཕྱིར། །རང་གི་དྲན་གསོར

2

གཉིས་

༄༅། །མཆན་གྱི་ངལ་འདི་བྱ། །ཞེས་ཡུལ་དམ་པ་རྣམས་ལ་ཤིས་པའི་མེ་ཏོག་ཉུང་ཟད་འཐོར་བས་ལེགས་བྱས་འདུ་བགྱིས་ནས། དེའང་བྱང་ཆུབ་སེམས་ཀྱི་བཀའ་བབ་ཆེན་པོ་དགེ་བཤེས་འཆད་ཁ་བ་ཡེ་ཤེས་རྡོ་རྗེས་མཛད་པའི། སྙིགས་དུས་ཀྱི་དམ་ཆོས་སྤྱོད་པ་ཡོངས་ལ་རྐྱེན་ངན་ལམ་འཁྱེར་གྱི་གདམས་ངག་བློ་སྦྱོང་དོན་བདུན་མ་ཞེས་བྱ་བ་ཅུང་ཟད་མཆན་བུས་དབྱེ་བ་ལ། སྔོན་འགྲོ་རྟེན་གྱི་ཆོས་བསྟན་པ། དངོས་གཞི་བྱང་ཆུབ་ཀྱི་སེམས་སྦྱོང་བ། རྐྱེན་ངན་བྱང་ཆུབ་ཀྱི་ལམ་དུ་བསྒྱུར་བ། ཚེ་གཅིག་གི་ཉམས་ལེན་དྲིལ་ནས་བསྟན་པ། བློ་འབྱོངས་པའི་ཚད། བློ་སྦྱོང་གི་དམ་

ཚིག བློ་སྦྱོང་གི་བསླབ་བྱ་བཅས་བདུན་ནོ། བློ་སྦྱོང་འདིའི་བརྒྱུད་པའི་ལོ་རྒྱུས་དང་། གདམས་པའི་ཆེ་བ་སོགས་ཞིབ་པར་འདོད་ན་བྱང་ཆུབ་ལམ་བཟང་སོགས་འགྲེལ་ཆེན་གཞན་ལས་རྟོགས་པར་བྱ་ཞིང་། མདོར་བསྡུས་ན། །མན་ངག་བདུད་རྩིའི་སྙིང་པོ་འདི། །གསེར་གླིང་པ་ནས་བརྒྱུད་པ་ཡིན། ཞེས་གསུངས་ཏེ། སྟོན་པ་མཆོག་དང་བྱམས་པ་ནས་བདག་གཞན་བརྗེ་བའི་བློ་སྦྱོང་གི་མན་ངག་ཟབ་མོ་སྙན་ནས་སྙན་དུ་བརྒྱུད་དེ་ཇོ་བོ་གསེར་གླིང་པ་དང་། བྱམས་སྙིང་རྗེ་བློ་སྦྱོང་སྦྱངས་པས་རང་གི་སྐུ་ཤ་གཞན་ཕྱོག་པ་ལ་སྟེར་ནུས་པ་བླ་མ་དྷརྨ་རཀྵི་ཏ་དང་། སེམས་ཅན་གྱི་སྡུག་བསྔལ་ལེན་ནུས་པ་བླ་མ་བྱམས་པའི་རྣལ་འབྱོར་པ་གསུམ་ལ་བཀའ་བབས་པ། དེ་གསུམ་ལས་ཇོ་བོ་རྗེས་གསན་པར་མཛད། སྤྱིར་ཇོ་བོ་ལ་མདོ་སྔགས་སྟོན་པའི་བླ་མ་བདུན་བཅུ་རྩ་གཉིས་བཞུགས་པ་ལས་ཐེག་པ་ཆེན་པོ་བློ་སྦྱོང་ཞུས་པའི་བླ་མ་འདི་གསུམ་གཙོ་བོ་མཛད། དེ་ལས་ཀྱང་བླ་མ་གཞན་གྱི་མཚན་གསུངས་པས་ཕྱག་ཐུགས་ཀར་ཐལ་མོ་སྦྱར། གསེར་གླིང་པའི་མཚན་འདོན་ཚེ་སྤྱན་ཆབ་གཡོ་ཞིང་ཐལ་མོ་སྤྱི་བོར་བཀོད་པ་སོགས་ཆེ་བཀུར་ཚད་མེད་མཛད། རྒྱུ་མཚན་ཞུས་པས། བདག་གཞན་བརྗེ་བའི་བྱང་ཆུབ་ཀྱི་སེམས་འདི་གསེར་

༄༅། །གླིང་པ་ཁོང་ལས་བྱུང་བའི་བཀའ་དྲིན་ཡིན་གསུངས། བོད་དུ་ཐེབས་ཏེ་རྒྱལ་འདིའི་ཆོས་ཀྱི་འཁོར་ལོ་བསྐོར་བ་ལས། ཇོ་བོ་གསེར་གླིང་པའི་བཀའ་སྲོལ་བློ་སྦྱོང་
ཐབ་མོ་རིམ་པར་བརྒྱུད་པ་འཆད་ཁ་བ་ཡེ་ཤེས་རྡོ་རྗེ་ལ་བཀར་བབས་ཏེ་དོན་བདུན་མ་འདི་མཛད་པའོ། །རྡོ་རྗེ་ཉི་མ་ལྷོན་ཤིང་བཞིན། །གཞུང་དོན་ལ་སོགས་ཤེས་པར་བྱ། ཅེས་གསུངས་པ་
ནི། རྡོ་རྗེ་རིན་པོ་ཆེས་རིན་པོ་ཆེ་གཞན་ཟིལ་གྱིས་གནོན་ཅིང་དབུལ་བ་སེལ་བ་དང་། ཉི་མའི་འོད་ཀྱིས་འོད་གཞན་ཟིལ་གྱིས་གནོན་ནས་མུན་པ་སེལ་བ་དང་། ལྷོན་གྱི་ལྷོན་ཤིང་གིས་ཤིང་
གཞན་ཟིལ་གྱིས་གནོན་ཅིང་ནད་སེལ་བ་ལྟར། བྱང་ཆུབ་སེམས་ཀྱིས་ཆོས་གཞན་ཟིལ་གྱིས་གནོན་ཏེ་སྡུག་བསྔལ་སེལ་ནས་ཕན་བདེ་བསྒྲུབ་པ་སྟེ། དཔེ་གསུམ་གྱིས་བློ་སྦྱོང་ཐབ་ཆོས་ཀྱི་
ཡོན་ཏན་བསྟན། སྙིགས་མ་ལྔ་པོ་བདོ་བ་འདི། །བྱང་ཆུབ་ལམ་དུ་བསྒྱུར་བ་ཡིན། ཅེས་གསུངས་པའི་དོན། དེང་སང་རྩོད་ལྡན་སྙིགས་མ་ལྔ་སྟོབས་ཤིན་ཏུ་ཆེ་བའི་དུས། ཆོས་གཞན་
གྱིས་རྐྱེན་ངན་མི་འདོད་པ་འདུལ་དཀའ་བ་ལ་བློ་སྦྱོང་སྒོམ་པས་བྱང་ཆུབ་ལམ་དུ་བསྒྱུར་བར་བྱེད་པ་ཡིན་ཏེ། དེ་དག་འོག་གི་གཞུང་དོན་ལས་རྟོགས་པར་བྱའོ། སྤྱིར་ཐེག་པ་གསུམ་གའང་བློ་ ༥

སྦྱོང་བའི་ཐབས་ཡིན་ཀྱང་སྐྱི་མིང་བྱེ་བྲག་ལ་བཏགས་ཏེ། གསེར་གླིང་པ་ནས་བརྒྱུད་པའི་བདག་གཞན་བརྗེ་བའི་གདམས་ངག་འདི་ལ་བློ་སྦྱོང་ཞེས་བརྗོད་དོ། དེ་ནི་གཞུང་དོན་ལས། །ཐོག་
མར་སྔོན་འགྲོ་དག་ལ་བསླབ། ཅེས་པས་འདི་ཉིད་སྔོན་ཐོག་གཅིག་ཏུ་བསྒོམ་པར་འདོད་པས། ཐོག་མར་སྔོན་དུ་འགྲོ་བའི་ཆོས་ནི། གང་དུ་བསྒྲུབ་པའི་གནས་སུ་གཙང་སྦྲ་དང་འབྱོར་ན་མཆོད་
པ་མཛེས་ཤིང་ཡིད་དུ་འོང་བ་བཀོད་ནས་ཡན་ལག་བདུན་པ་སོགས་ལེགས་པར་བྱས་ཏེ། སྐྱན་ལ་བདེ་བར་འདུག་ཅིང་ཐེག་པ་ཆེ་ཆུང་ཐུན་མོང་གི་ཀུན་སློང་དག་ལ་བསླབ་པར་བྱ་སྟེ། དལ་
འབྱོར་རྙེད་དཀའ། འཆི་བ་མི་རྟག་པ། ལས་རྒྱུ་འབྲས། འཁོར་བའི་ཉེས་དམིགས་སོགས་གསལ་བཏབ་སྟེ་བློ་ཆོས་ལ་བསྐྱུལ། དེ་ནས་ཐུན་མིན་སྔོན་འཇུག་གི་སེམས་བཟུང་བ་ལ་སྐྱབས་
འགྲོ་དང་ཚད་མེད་བཞི་སོགས་བྱས་ལ། བདག་གིས་སེམས་ཅན་ཐམས་ཅད་ཀྱི་དོན་དུ་མྱུར་བར་ཡང་དག་པར་རྫོགས་པའི་སངས་རྒྱས་ཀྱི་གོ་འཕང་ཐོབ་པར་བྱ། དེའི་ཆེད་དུ་ཐེག་པ་ཆེན་
པོའི་བློ་སྦྱོང་གི་གདམས་པ་ཟབ་མོ་ཉམས་སུ་ལེན་པར་བགྱིའོ། ཞེས་ལན་གསུམ་དང་། དེ་ནས་བླ་མ་དངོས་སམ། སྤྱི་ལ་རྒྱལ་བ་ཐམས་ཅད་ཀྱི་སྙིང་རྗེའི་རང་གཟུགས། ལྷ་ཡི་སྐུར་ཤར ༦

༄༅། །བ་འཕགས་མཆོག་ཕྱག་ན་སྒོམ་ཉིད་སྒོམ་ན་ལེགས་ཅེས་གསུངས་པས། རང་གི་སྤྱི་བོར་པད་ཟླའི་གདན་ལ་ངོ་བོ་རང་གི་རྩ་བའི་བླ་མ་ལ་རྣམ་པ་འཕགས་པ་སྤྱན་
རས་གཟིགས་གསལ་བའི་སྐུ་ལས་འོད་ཟེར་དཀར་པོ་མཁའ་ཁྱབ་ཏུ་འཕྲོ་ཞིང་། ཐུགས་དམིགས་མེད་སྙིང་རྗེས་འགྲོ་ལ་དགོངས་ཏེ་བཞུགས་པ་སྐྱབས་གནས་ཀུན་འདུས་ཀྱི་ངོ་བོར་བསམ། བློ་
སྦྱོང་བརྒྱུད་པའི་གསོལ་འདེབས་དང་ཁྱད་པར་དུ། །བླ་མ་ཡང་དག་པ་ཡོངས་ཀྱི་དགེ་བའི་བཤེས་གཉེན་ཆེན་པོས་བདག་ལ་བྱིན་གྱིས་བརླབ་ཏུ་གསོལ། བྱམས་སྙིང་རྗེ་བྱང་ཆུབ་ཀྱི་
སེམས་ཁྱད་པར་ཅན་རྒྱུད་ལ་སྐྱེ་བར་མཛད་དུ་གསོལ། ཞེས་ལན་བརྒྱ་སྟོང་དང་། ཇོ་བོ་རྗེའི་གསོལ་འདེབས་འབྲོམ་སྟོན་པས་གསུངས་པ། །ཤིན་ཏུ་ལེགས་པ་ངོ་མཚར་རྒྱ་མཚོའི་
དཔལ༔ །ཀུན་ལ་བྱང་སེམས་འབྱོངས་བར་བྱིན་གྱིས་རློབས། །རྒྱལ་རིགས་རིག་པའི་གནས་ལྔ་ཀུན་ལ་མཁས། །སློལ་མས་ལུང་བསྟན་གངས་ཅན་དཔལ་དུ་བྱོན། །བདག་བས
གཞན་གཅེས་འབྱོངས་ནས་གཞན་དོན་མཛད། །མཚུངས་མེད་ཨ་ཏི་ཤ་ལ་གསོལ་བ་འདེབས། །ད་ལྟ་ཉིད་དུ་བྱིན་གྱིས་བརླབ་ཏུ་གསོལ། །སྐྱེ་རྒུའི་སྡུག་བསྔལ་འཕྲུལ་དུ་བསལ་དུ་
གསོལ༔ །འགྲོ་ཀུན་བྱང་ཆུབ་ལམ་དུ་དྲང་དུ་གསོལ། །ཕན་བདེ་ཀུན་གྱི་འབྱུང་གནས་སྨྲུལ་དུ་གསོལ། །སྲིད་འགོག་ད་ལྟ་ཉིད་དུ་འཇུག་ཏུ་གསོལ། །བདེ་འགོ་དེ་རིང་ཉིད་ནས་སྨྲུལ་དུ་
གསོལ༔ །སྲིད་པའི་སྡུག་བསྔལ་ཐམས་ཅད་གཞོམ་དུ་གསོལ། །ཆོས་ཀྱི་བར་ཅད་ཐམས་ཅད་བཟློག་ཏུ་གསོལ། །བྲྀ་རྒྱུ་ཆོས་ལས་མེད་པར་བྱིན་གྱིས་རློབས། །ཞེས་སོགས་མོས་གུས་
ཤུགས་དྲག་མ་སྐྱེས་བར་དུ། སྙིང་ཐག་པ་ནས་གསོལ་བ་བཏབ་པའི་མཐར། བླ་མ་སྤྱན་རས་གཟིགས་རང་གི་སྤྱི་བོའི་ཚངས་བུག་ནས་མར་བྱོན་ཏེ་སྙིང་འོད་ཀྱི་གུར་ཁང་གི་དབུས་སུ་པད་ཟླའི་
གདན་ལ་དགྱེས་འཛུམ་ཡེ་རེ་བཞུགས་པའི་ཐུགས་དང་རང་གི་སེམས་དབྱེར་མེད་དུ་བསམ་སྟེ་དལ་ཅིག་མཉམ་པར་འཇོག་པ་ནི་ཐུན་འགོ་ཐབས་ཅད་ལ་བྱའོ། དེ་ལ་བླ་མ་དངོས་སྒོམ་པར
གསུངས་པའང་། དགེ་བཤེས་སྤྱིལ་བུ་པས་མཛད་པའི་བློ་སྦྱོང་བླ་མའི་རྣལ་འབྱོར་ལས། སློབ་མ་ལ་བརྩོན་འགྲུས་དང་ཡོན་ཏན་སོགས་ཡོད་ཀྱང་བླ་མ་བྱིན་རླབས་དང་ལྡན་པ་ལ་མ་བསྟེན
པར་རྟོགས་པ་མི་སྐྱེ་བས། བླ་མ་དམ་པ་བསྟེན་དགོས་ལ་མཚན་ཉིད་ཀྱང་། །བླ་མའི་མཚན་ཉིད་བརྒྱུད་པར་ལྡན། །རྟོགས་པ་ཡོད་ན་ཚད་ལྡན་ཡིན། ཅེས་རྗོགས་པའི་སངས་རྒྱས་ནས

ཅྱི

༄༅། །བརྒྱུད་པ་བརམ་ཆད་པར་བྱང་ཆུབ་སེམས་ལ་ངེས་པོ་བཏན་པོ་ཡོད་པ་ཇོ་བོའི་བཀའ་བརྒྱུད་ལྟ་བུ་ལ་བསྟེན་དགོས། དོན་གྱི་སྒོ་ནས་བསྟེན་པ་བླ་མས་ཇི་ལྟར་
གསུངས་པ་སྒོ་གསུམ་གྱིས་བསླབས་པ་ཡིན། གསང་བ་བཟད་འི་སྒོ་ནས་བསྟན་པ་ནི་རང་གི་སྙིང་གའམ་སྤྱི་གཙུག་ཏུ་བླ་མ་བསྒོམས་ནས་མོས་གུས་དྲུས་གསོལ་བ་འདེབས་པ་ཡིན་སོགས་
གསུངས་པས་ཤེས་སོ། །དེ་ནས་ལུས་དྲང་པོར་བསྲང་སྟེ་དབུགས་ཕྱིར་རྒྱུ་བ་དང་ནང་དུ་རྔུབས་པ་ལ་སེམས་གཏད་ནས་དལ་བུས་ལན་ཉེར་གཅིག་གི་བར་དུ་བགྲངས་སྟེ་རླུང་སེམས་རྣལ་དུ་
དབབ་ཏེ་བསམ་གཏན་གྱི་སྣོད་དུ་རུང་བར་བྱ། དེ་ནས་དངོས་གཞི་བློ་སྦྱོང་གི་ཚིག་དོན་རེ་རེ་བཞིན་རང་རྒྱུད་ལ་འཕོལ་ངེས་བསྒོམ་པར་བྱ་སྟེ། དེའང་ཕྱི་གཟུང་བའི་ཡུལ་བདེན་པར་མ་གྲུབ་
སྟེ། །ཆོས་རྣམས་རྨི་ལམ་ལྟ་བུར་བསམ། ཞེས་པས་ཚོགས་དྲུག་གི་ཡུལ་དུ་སྣང་བའི་ཆོས་རྣམས་ནི། རང་རང་གི་ལས་བཟང་ངན་གྱི་སྣང་ཆ་ཙམ་ལས་དོན་དུ་བདེན་པར་མ་གྲུབ་པ་རྨི་
ལམ་གྱི་སྣོད་བཅུད་ལྟ་བུ་སྣང་ན་མི་བདེན་པ་འཁྲུལ་པ་ཡིན་པ་ལ་ཁྱད་མེད་པར་བསམ་ལ་འདུན་པ་ཡང་ཡང་སྦྱང་། དེའི་ཚེ། འོ་ན་ཕྱི་ཡུལ་དུ་འཁྲུལ་མཁན་གྱི་ནང་འཛིན་པའི་སེམས་འདི་

9

བདེན་ནམ་སྙམ་ན། །མ་སྐྱེས་རིག་པའི་གཤིས་ལ་དཔྱད། ཅེས་པས་སེམས་འདི་ཡང་དཔྱད་ན་བདེན་པར་མ་གྲུབ་སྟེ་དང་པོ་བྱུང་སའི་ཁུངས་མེད་པས་མ་སྐྱེས། བར་དུ་རང་གི་ལུས་ཀྱི་ཕྱི་
ནང་གང་ལའང་མི་གནས། མཐར་འགག་པའི་ཡུལ་མེད་པའི་སེམས་སྟོང་པ་གསལ་ཙམ་གྱི་རིག་པའི་ངོ་བོའམ་གཤིས་དེ་ལ་དཔྱད་དེ་སྟོང་ཉིད་སྤྲོས་བྲལ་ནམ་མཁའ་ལྟ་བུར་གཏན་ལ་ཕབ།
དེའི་ཚེ་སེམས་སྟོང་ཉིད་ལ། སྟོང་པར་ཞེན་ཏེ་གཉེན་པོའི་འཛིན་པ་བྱུང་ན། །གཉེན་པོ་ཉིད་ཀྱང་རང་སར་གྲོལ། ཞེས་པས་སྒོམ་མཁན་གཉེན་པོ་སྟོང་པར་འཛིན་པའི་དྲན་པ་དེ་ཉིད་ཀྱང་གཏད་
མེད་ཀྱི་ངང་དུ་རང་སར་གྲོལ་བར་བྱས་ཏེ་མ་ཡེངས་པར་འཇོག་པ་འཁོར་གསུམ་དམིགས་པ་མེད་པའི་ཤེས་རབ་སྟེ། འདི་ཡན་དཔྱད་སྒོམ་དང་། དེ་ནས་འཇོག་སྒོམ་ལ། །ངོ་བོ་ཀུན་གཞིའི་
ངང་ལ་བཞག ཅེས་པས་བཟང་ངན་གྱི་རྣམ་རྟོག་གང་གིས་ཀྱང་མ་བསླད་པའི་ངོ་བོ་གཉུག་མ་ཀུན་གཞིའི་རང་ངོ་གསལ་ལ་མི་རྟོག་པའི་ངང་ལ་བྱིང་རྒོད་སོགས་དང་བྲལ་བར་འཇོག །རྗེ་
བཙུན་མི་ལས། ཀུན་གཞིའི་ངོས་འཛིན་ལ། འོ་སྐོལ་སེམས་ཅན་རྣམས་ཀྱི་སེམས་འོད་གསལ་སྟོང་པ་འཁོར་འདས་ཀྱི་སྤྱི་ཡིན་གང་གིས་ཀྱང་མ་གོས་པ་འདི་ལ་ཀུན་གཞིའི་སངས་རྒྱས་

10

༦ཀ

༄༅། །ཞེས་ཀྱང་བྱ། རང་ངོ་རང་གིས་ཤེས་ཤིང་རིག་པ་ལ་ཡེ་ཤེས་བྱ། གསུངས་པ་བཞིན་ནོ། གང་ལྟར་དེ་ནི་འཇོག་སྒོམ་སྟེ་མཉམ་བཞག་ཐུན་གྱི་དངོས་གཞིའི་
སྐབས་ཀྱི་སྐྱོང་ཚུལ་དང་། རྗེས་ཐོབ་ལ། །ཐུན་མཚམས་སྒྱུ་མའི་སྐྱེས་བུར་བྱ། །ཞེས་པས་ཐུན་མཚམས་ཟ་ཉལ་འགྲོ་འདུག་སོགས་སྤྱོད་ལམ་ཐམས་ཅད་དུ་མཉམ་བཞག་སྐབས་ཀྱི་དྲན་པ་
མ་བརྗེད་པའི་ངང་ནས་རང་གཞན་སྣོད་བཅུད་ཐམས་ཅད་དོན་ལ་མེད་བཞིན་སྣང་བ་སྒྱུ་མའི་སྐྱེས་བུ་ལྟར་ཐམས་ཅད་ལ་བདེན་ཞེན་སྤང་བར་བྱ་ཞིང་ལམ་དུ་འཁྱེར། འདི་ཡན་དོན་དམ་བྱང་ཆུབ་
ཀྱི་སེམས་སྒོམ་ཚུལ་དང་། དེ་ནས་ཀུན་རྫོབ་བྱང་ཆུབ་ཀྱི་སེམས་སྒོམ་པའི་སྐབས་ལ་དངོས་གཞི་གཏོང་ལེན་སྒོམ་པ་ཡིན་པས་སྒོམ་ཡུལ་སྡུག་བསྔལ་གྱིས་མནར་བའི་སེམས་ཅན་ཐམས་ཅད་
མར་ཤེས་དྲིན་དྲན་དགོས་པས། ཐོག་མར་རང་གི་མའི་དྲིན་ལེགས་པར་བསམ་ཞིང་དེ་ཡིས་སེམས་ཅན་དེ་དག་ལ་བཀབ་ནས་ཐམས་ཅད་རང་གི་མ་ཡིན་པའི་བློ་བཅོས་མིན་དུ་བསྐྱེད་ནས་དེ་
དག་ལ་བྱམས་དང་སྙིང་རྗེའི་ངང་ནས། །གཏོང་ལེན་གཉིས་པོ་སྤེལ་མར་སྦྱང་ས། །དེ་ཉིད་རླུང་ལ་བསྐྱོན་ཏེ་བྱ། ཞེས་པས། བདག་གཞན་བརྗེ་བའི་བྱང་ཆུབ་སེམས་ནི་བློ་སྦྱོང་ཆོས་ཀྱི་

11

སྙིང་པོ་ཡིན་པའི་ཕྱིར། བདག་གི་ལུས་ལོངས་སྤྱོད་དུས་གསུམ་གྱི་དགེ་བ་དང་བདེ་བ་ཐམས་ཅད་གཞན་སེམས་ཅན་ལ་གཏོང་ཞིང་། དེ་རྣམས་ཀྱི་སྡུག་བསྔལ་རྒྱུ་འབྲས་དང་བཅས་པ་ཐམས་
ཅད་ཁོ་ལ་ལྷག་མ་མེད་པར་བདག་གིས་ལེན་པར་བགྱིའོ་སྙམ་པའི་དམིགས་རྣམ་གཉིས་པོ་ཆའམ་སྤེལ་མར་སྦྱངས་དགོས་ཤིང་དེ་དག་གོམས་པའི་ཚེད་དུ་བདེ་སྡུག་གི་དངོས་པོ་དེ་ཉིད་ཀྱང་རང་
གི་དབུགས་ཀྱི་རླུང་ལ་བསྐྱོན་ཏེ་བསྒོམ་པར་བྱ་སྟེ། དམིགས་པ་གསལ་བའི་ཁྲིད་དབུགས་ནང་དུ་བརྡུབས་པ་དང་། དེ་དག་གི་སྡིག་སྒྲིབ་སྡུག་བསྔལ་ཐམས་ཅད་ནག་ཝུབ་ཀྱིས་སྣ་སྒོ་དང་བ
སྤྱིའི་བུ་ག་ནས་རང་གི་སྙིང་ནང་བདག་འཛིན་གྱི་ཐོག་ཏུ་འམ། ཡི་དམ་གཞན་ནམ་སྤྱན་རས་གཟིགས་ལྟ་བུ་སྒོམ་པའི་སྐབས་ཡིན་ན། རང་ཉིད་སྤྱན་རས་གཟིགས་སུ་གསལ་བ་ལ་ཐིམ་པས་
གངས་རིའི་ཕུང་པོ་ལ་ཉི་འོད་ཐོག་པ་ལྟར་དཀར་འཚེར་གཟི་བྱིན་སྤར་ལས་འབར་བར་བསམ། རིགས་དྲུག་གི་སེམས་ཅན་ཐམས་ཅད་ཀྱི་སྡིག་པ་དག་ཅིང་རང་རང་གི་སྡུག་བསྔལ་གང་ཡོད་པ
ལས་གྲོལ་སོང་སྙམ་པའི་སྙིང་རྗེ་ཚད་མེད་བསྐྱེད། དབུགས་ཕྱིར་རྒྱུ་བ་དང་སྣ་སྒོ་དང་བ་སྤྱིའི་བུ་ག་ནས་དཀར་ལམ་གྱིས་སོང་སྟེ་རིགས་དྲུག་སོ་སོའི་ལུས་དང་གནས་ལ་ཐིམ་པས། རང་གི་

12

༄༅། །བདེ་བ་དང་དགེ་བ་ཐམས་ཅད་རིགས་དྲུག་སོ་སོར་ཅི་མཁོ་བ། རྒྱ་ཆེ་ཞིང་ཟད་མི་ཤེས་པ་ནམ་མཁའ་མཛོད་དུ་གྱུར་ནས་དེ་རྣམས་སྡུག་བསྔལ་དང་བྲལ་ནས་གནས་སྐབས་ལུས་སེམས་བདེ་སྐྱིད་དང་ལྡན། མཐར་ཐུག་སངས་རྒྱས་ཀྱི་གོ་འཕང་ཐོབ་སོང་སྙམ་སྟེ་བྱམས་པ་ཚད་མེད་བསྐྱེད། འདི་ཉིད་མཉམ་གཞག་ཐུན་གྱི་དངོས་གཞི་རྒྱ་ཞིང་སྤྱོད་ལམ་ཐམས་ཅད་ལ་འང་བསྒོམ་པར་བྱ། གཏོང་ལེན་འདི་ནི་སེམས་བཟུང་སླ་བ་དང་། འབྱོངས་སྐྱེན་པ་དང་། རྣམ་རྟོག་མང་པོ་གཅུན་པའི་ཆེད་དུ་མཛད་པ་ཡིན་གསུངས། འདི་ནི་ཚད་མེད་བཞིའི་སྙིང་པོའང་ཡིན་ཏེ། གཏོང་བ་ནི་བྱམས་པ་ཚད་མེད། ལེན་པ་ནི་སྙིང་རྗེ་ཚད་མེད། སེམས་ཅན་ཐམས་ཅད་ཀྱི་སྡུག་བསྔལ་བསལ་ཞིང་བདེ་ལ་བཀོད་པར་དམིགས་པ་དགའ་བ་ཚད་མེད། དགྲ་གཉེན་ཡོངས་ལ་ཉེ་རིང་མེད་པར་སྒོམ་པ་བཏང་སྙོམས་ཚད་མེད་དོ། ཁ་ཅིག་གིས། གཞན་གྱི་སྡུག་བསྔལ་ལེན་ན་རང་ལ་མི་གནོད་དམ་ཟེར། །དེ་ལྟར་ལན་རྒྱུ་ཞིག་མཆིས་ན། དགེ་བཤེས་འཆད་ཁ་ལྟ་བུ་བདག་གཞན་བརྗེ་བའི་བྱང་ཆུབ་ཀྱི་སེམས་ཁྱད་པར་ཅན་འབྱོངས་ནས་བདག་གཅེས་འཛིན་གཏན་ནས་ཟད་པ་ན། ཞི་བ་ལྷས། །པད་མའི་མཚོ་རུ་ངང་པ་བཞིན། །

མནར་མེད་པར་ཡང་འཇུག་པར་འགྱུར། གསུངས་པ་ལྟར་གཞན་གྱི་སྡུག་བསྔལ་རང་ལ་བླངས་ནས་སྤྱོད་འདོད་ཀྱི་གཏོང་ལེན་ཁྱད་པར་ཅན་འབྱོངས་ན་གཞན་བདེ་བའི་ཆེད་དུ་རང་ལ་སེམས་ཅན་ཐམས་ཅད་ཀྱི་སྡུག་བསྔལ་དུས་གཅིག་ཏུ་སྨྱོང་ཡང་འདོད་ཐོག་ཏུ་འགྱུར་པར་སྙམ། འོན་ཀྱང་རིགས་དྲུག་གི་སེམས་ཅན་རྣམས་ཀྱིས་ལས་ངན་བསགས་པའི་རྣམ་པར་སྨིན་པ་མ་རྫོགས་བར་དུ་རང་རང་གི་བྱས་པའི་ཕུང་པོ་ལ་སྨྱོང་བ་ལས་གཞན་ལ་སྤོ་ཐབས་མེད་གསུངས་པས་ཤེས་སོ། གཞན་ཡང་བསམ་དགོས་པ་ནི། སྟོན་གྱི་སངས་རྒྱས་རྣམས་ཀྱིས་གཏོང་ལེན་མཛད་ནས་སེམས་ཅན་ཐམས་ཅད་ཀྱི་སྡིག་སྒྲིབ་དང་སྡུག་བསྔལ་སྐུ་ལ་སྨྱོང་བ་ལྟ་ཅི། དེ་འདྲའི་སྙིང་རྗེའི་གཏོང་ལེན་གྱི་ཐུགས་ལ་བསྟེན་ནས་བདེ་སྐྱིད་ཀྱི་མཐར་ཐུག་པ་ལམ་ལྔ་ས་བཅུའི་ཕ་མཐར་བླ་ན་མེད་པའི་གོ་འཕང་དུ་གཤེགས་པ་ཡིན་པས། རང་ཅག་རྣམས་ཀྱང་དེ་ལྟ་བུའི་གོ་འཕང་ཐོབ་པ་ལ་ཐབས་སྙིང་རྗེ་ཆེན་པོ་ལས་ལྷག་པ་མེད་པར་གསུངས་ཤིང་། དེ་ཡི་སྙིང་པོའང་གཏོང་ལེན་སྒོམ་པ་ཡིན་ཏེ། འཇམ་དབྱངས་ས་སྐྱ་པཎྜི་ཏས། །ཁ་ཅིག་བརྗེ་བའི་བྱང་ཆུབ་སེམས། །བསྒོམ་དུ་མི་རུང་ཞེས་སུ་སྨྲ། །དེ་དོན་འདི་ལྟར་བསམ་པར་བྱ། །བདག་གཞན་བརྗེ་བའི་བྱང་ཆུབ་

༄༅། །སེམས༔ །དགེ་བ་ཡིན་ནམ་སྡིག་ཡིན་བརྟག །གལ་ཏེ་དགེ་བ་ཡིན་ན་ནི། །དེ་ལས་སྡུག་བསྔལ་འབྱུང་བ་འགལ། །སྡིག་པ་ཡིན་ན་དུག་གསུམ་གྱིས། །
བསྐྱེད་པའི་ལས་སུ་ཐལ་བར་འགྱུར། །བརྗེ་བ་དུག་གསུམ་མ་ཡིན་པས། །དེ་ལས་སྡུག་བསྔལ་ག་ལ་འབྱུང་། །བྱང་ཆུབ་སེམས་དཔའི་བློ་སྦྱོང་བའི། །སློན་ལམ་འགའ་ཞིག་མཐའ་མི་
བཙན༔ །གལ་ཏེ་བཙན་ན་མཇའ་བོའི་བུ། །རྒྱུན་དུ་ཟླད་ནད་ཆེན་པོར་འགྱུར། །དུས་གསུམ་སངས་རྒྱས་ཐམས་ཅད་ཀྱང་། །བདག་གཞན་བརྗེ་བ་སྒོམ་པའི་ཕྱིར། །རྒྱུན་དུ་སྡུག་བསྔལ་
ཐོབ་པར་འགྱུར། །བརྗེས་པའི་སེམས་ཅན་དེ་དག་ཀུན། །སྡུག་བསྔལ་འབྱུང་བ་སྲིད་མི་འགྱུར། །དེས་ན་འདི་འདྲའི་གསང་ཚིག་ནི། །བདུད་ཀྱི་ཡིན་པ་ཤེས་པར་བྱ། །བདག་གཞན་བརྗེ་
བ་སངས་རྒྱས་ཀྱི། །བསྟན་པའི་སྙིང་པོ་ཡིན་པར་གསུངས། །ཞེས་བླ་མ་འཇམ་པའི་དབྱངས་ཀྱིས་གསུངས་པ་བཞིན། འདི་འདྲའི་ཉམས་ལེན་བྱ་རྒྱུ་ཡོད་པ་དགའ་བ་བསྒོམ་པར་བྱའོ། བློ་
སྦྱོང་ཐུན་དུ་བཟུང་བའི་སྐབས། ཐུན་གྱི་དངོས་གཞི། ཞི་ལྷག་གི་ཏིང་ངེ་འཛིན་དང་། ཁྲིད་པར་གཏོང་ལེན་ལ་འབད་ཅིང་། འདི་སྐབས་ཐང་སྟོང་རྒྱལ་པོས་མཛད་པའི་སྨྱུན་རས་གཟིགས་ཀྱི

སྒོམ་བཟླས་འགྲོ་དོན་མཁའ་ཁྱབ་མ་དམིགས་བཟླས་བྱ་ཞིང་ཡིག་དྲུག་བཟླ་སྐབས་གཏོང་ལེན་དམིགས་པ་བྱ་བའང་ཡོད། ཐུན་གྱི་མཇུག་ཏུ་བློ་སྦྱོང་སྨོན་ལམ་རྒྱས་བསྡུས་ཅི་རིགས་པ་དང་།
བཟང་སྤྱོད་སོགས་བསྔོ་སྨོན་གྱིས་རྒྱས་འདེབས། འདི་ནི་བློ་སྦྱོང་ཉམས་ལེན་དུས་སུ། ཐུན་ནམ་མཉམ་གཞག་གི་སྐབས་ཡིན་ཅིང་། རྗེས་ཐོབ་བམ། ཐུན་མཚམས་སོགས་རྒྱུན་དུ་ཚིག
སྐྱོར་ཞིང་དོན་ལ་ཉམས་ལེན་བྱེད་རྒྱུ་གལ་ཤིན་ཏུ་ཆེ་བ་ལ། །ཡུལ་གསུམ་དུག་གསུམ་དགེ་རྩ་གསུམ། ཞེས་པས་ཡུལ་སེམས་ཅན་དང་བེམ་པོའི་དངོས་པོ་རང་གི་ཡིད་དུ་འོང་བ་ལ་སྲིད་ཞེན
དང་བརྣབ་སེམས། སེར་སྣ། བརྒྱ་སེམས་སོགས་འདོད་ཆགས། དེ་བཞིན་དགྲ་འདྲེ་སོགས་ཡུལ་ཡིད་དུ་མི་འོང་པ་ལ་ཁོང་ཁྲོ། གནོད་སེམས། འཁོན་འཛིན། རྩུན་དང་ཕྲམ། ཚིག
རྩུབ༔ འཁྲུག་ལྷ་སོགས་ཞེ་སྡང་། ཡུལ་སེམས་ཅན་སོགས་བར་མ་ལ་ཕན་གནོད་ཀྱི་བསམ་པ་གང་ཡང་མེད་ཅིང་བདེན་འཛིན་ངང་བཏང་སྙོམས་སུ་ལུས་པའི་གཏི་མུག་སྟེ། དེ་གསུམ་ནི་རང་
གཞན་ལ་སྡུག་བསྔལ་བསྐྱེད་པའི་རྩ་བ་དུག་རྫས་ལྟ་བུ་གསུམ་ཡིན་པ་ཤེས་ནས་སྤྱངས་ཅི་ཐུབ་ཀྱིས་དེ་གསུམ་དགེ་བའི་རྩ་བ་གསུམ་ལ་བསྒྱུར་བའི་ཐབས་ནི། བྱང་ཆུབ་གཞུང་ལམ་དུ།

དགུ

༄༅། །འདོད་ཆགས་སྐྱེས་པའི་ཚེ། སེམས་ཅན་ཐམས་ཅད་ཀྱི་ཉོན་མོངས་པ་འདོད་ཆགས་ཇི་སྙེད་པ་ཐབས་ཅད་བདག་གི་འདི་ལ་འདུས་པར་གྱུར་ཅིག སེམས་ཅན་ཐམས་ཅད་འདོད་ཆགས་མེད་པའི་དགེ་རྩ་དང་ལྡན་པར་གྱུར་ཅིག དེ་རྣམས་ཀྱི་ཉོན་མོངས་པའི་གོ་བདག་གི་འདིས་ཚོད་ནས་སངས་རྒྱས་མ་ཐོབ་ཀྱི་བར་དུ་ཉོན་མོངས་པ་དང་བྲལ་བར་གྱུར་ཅིག དེ་བཞིན་དུ་ཞེ་སྡང་སྐྱེས་པའི་ཚེ། སེམས་ཅན་ཐམས་ཅད་ཀྱི་ཉོན་མོངས་པ་ཞེ་སྡང་ཇི་སྙེད་པ་ཐམས་ཅད༔ བྲལ་བར་གྱུར་ཅིག བར་དང་། གཏི་མུག་སྐྱེས་པའི་ཚེ། སེམས་ཅན་ཐམས་ཅད་ཀྱི་ཉོན་མོངས་པ་གཏི་མུག་ཇི་སྙེད་པ་ཐམས་ཅད༔ བྲལ་བར་གྱུར་ཅིག གསུངས་པ་རྣམས་ངག་གིས་བརྗོད་ཅིང་བསམ་སྟེ། མི་དགེ་བ་ཉོན་མོངས་པ་དུག་གསུམ་དེ་ལྟར་དགེ་བའི་སེམས་གཉེན་ལེན་གྱི་ལམ་དུ་བསྒྱུར་བས་དེ་གསུམ་དགེ་བའི་རྩ་བ་རྒྱ་ཆེན་པོ་གསུམ་དུ་འགྱུར་བ་དེ་བཞིན་དུ་ཉོན་མོངས་པ་ང་རྒྱལ། ཕྲག་དོག སེར་སྣ་སོགས་སྐྱེས་པའི་ཚེ་གོང་བཞིན་ཁ་བསྒྱུར་ན་ལེགས། འདི་ནི་མི་གཙང་བ་ཤ་ཕང་གཅིའི་ཕུང་པོ་ཞིང་ཁར་ལུད་དུ་བླུགས་པས་ལོ་ཏོག་བཟང་པོ་སྐྱེ་བའི་རྒྱུར་འགྱུར་བ་བཞིན་ནོ། དེ་བཞིན་གུ་རུ་རིན་པོ་ཆེས། འདི་ལྟར་ཡིད་ཀྱི་

17

ཡུལ་དུ་འགྱུ་བ་ཡི། །ཉོན་མོངས་དུག་ལྔའི་རྟོག་པ་ཅི་ཤར་ཡང་། །སྔོན་བསུ་རྗེས་དཔྱོད་བློ་ཡིས་བཅོས་མི་གཞུག །འགྱུ་བ་རང་སར་བཞག་པས་ཆོས་སྐུར་གྲོལ། ཅེས་སྤངས་བླངས་མེད་པར་རང་གྲོལ་ཏུ་ཐད་ཀར་བཞག་པས་ཡེ་ཤེས་སུ་བསྒྱུར་བའི་ཐབས་གསུངས་པའང་གནད་གཅིག་པའོ། །དེ་ལ་དྲན་པ་བསྐུལ་བའི་ཕྱིར་དུ། །སྤྱོད་ལམ་ཀུན་ཏུ་ཚིག་གིས་སྦྱོང་། ཞེས་པས་ཟ་ཉལ་འགྲོ་འདུག་སོགས་སྤྱོད་ལམ་ཀུན་ཏུ་ཚིག་གིས་ཤུབ་བུའམ་གདངས་དང་བཅས་སྦྱོང་སྟེ། །འགྲོ་བའི་སྡུག་བསྔལ་གང་ཅི་རུང་། །དེ་ཀུན་བདག་ལ་སྨིན་གྱུར་ཅིག །བྱང་ཆུབ་སེམས་དཔའི་དགེ་འདུན་གྱིས། །འགྲོ་བ་བདེ་ལ་སྤྱོད་པར་ཤོག །སྐྱིད་ན་བདེ་བ་ཚོགས་སུ་བསྔོ། །ཕན་བདེའི་ནམ་མཁའ་གང་བར་ཤོག །སྡུག་ན་ཀུན་གྱི་སྡུག་བསྔལ་ཁུར། །སྡུག་བསྔལ་གྱི་རྒྱ་མཚོ་སྐེམ་པར་ཤོག ཅེས་དང་། །བདག་ལ་དེ་དག་སྡིག་སྨིན་ཅིང་། །བདག་དགེ་མ་ལུས་དེར་སྨིན་ཤོག ཅེས་དང་། །གང་ཞིག་བདག་དང་གཞན་རྣམས་ནི། །མྱུར་དུ་བསྐྱབ་པར་འདོད་པ་དེས། །བདག་དང་གཞན་དུ་བརྗེ་བྱ་བ། །གསང་བའི་དམ་པ་སྤྱད་པར་བྱ། ཞེས་སོགས་རྒྱལ་སྲས་ཞི་བ་ལྷས་གསུངས་ཤིང་། གསང་བའི་དམ་པ་ནི། བདག་གཞན་བརྗེ་བའི་བསམ་པ་

18

༄༅། །སྐབས་པོ་ཆེ་འདིའི་མན་ངག་གི་གནད་རྣམས་གདུལ་བྱ་བློ་གྲོས་ཆུང་བ་རྣམས་ཀྱི་བློར་མི་ཤོང་ཞིང་རྗེས་སུ་ཡི་རངས་ཙམ་ཡང་བྱ་དཀའ་བའི་གནས་ཡིན་པས
གསང་བར་བྱ་དགོས་གསུངས། ཡང་གསང་བའི་དམ་པའི་དོན་གཞན་ནི། གཏོང་ལེན་ནམ་དོན་དམ་བྱང་ཆུབ་སེམས་ལ་བཞེད་པའང་མཆིས། རྗེ་རིན་པོ་ཆེས། །བདག་བས་གཞན
གཅེས་སློམ་པའི་བྱང་ཆུབ་སེམས། །ལྷག་བསམ་དག་པ་རྒྱུད་ལ་བསྐྱེད་བྱས་ནས། །བླ་མེད་བྱང་ཆུབ་གོ་འཕང་སྟེར་བར་ཤོག ཅེས་དམ་པ་རྣམས་ཀྱི་གསུངས་རང་གིས་གང་ཐོན་སྒྲོར་བར
བྱས་ནས་དོན་གསལ་འདེབས་ཤུགས་དྲག་བྱ་ཞིང་། །ཡིན་པའི་གོ་རིམས་རང་ནས་བརྩམ། ཞེས་པས་གཞན་གྱི་སྡུག་བསྔལ་ལེན་པའི་གོ་རིམས་ཀྱང་། གོམས་པའི་ཆེད་དུ་ཐོག་མ་ར་རང
གི་སྡུག་བསྔལ་ལེན་པ་ནས་བརྩམ་དགོས་པས། རང་གི་སྐྱེ་བ་ཕྱི་མ་སོགས་དང་དེ་རིང་ཕན་ཆད་དུ་སྨིན་པར་འགྱུར་བའི་སྡུག་བསྔལ་རྒྱུ་དང་བཅས་པ་ཐམས་ཅད་ད་ལྟའི་ལུས་འདིའི་སྟེང་དུ
བསྡུས་ནས་བདག་གཅེས་པར་འཛིན་པའི་བློ་འདིའི་ཐོག་ཏུ་འདུས་ཤིང་སྨིན་ནས། བདག་དང་བདག་གིར་འཛིན་པ་སོགས་གཞི་མེད་འཁྲུལ་པའི་མ་རིག་པ་ཐལ་བར་བརླགས་ནས་བདག་མེད

རྟོགས་པའི་ཤེས་རབ་སྐྱེས་པར་བསམ། འདི་བྱང་ནས་གཙོད་གཞན་གྱི་སྡུག་བསྔལ་རྣམས་བླང་དགོས་པར་གསུངས། འོ་ན་བདག་ལ་གཅེས་འཛིན་བྱ་མི་རིགས་སམ་ཞེ་ན། སྡུག་བསྔལ་གྱི
རྟེན་དུ་གྱུར་པའི་བདག་གམ། ང་ནི་གཏན་ནས་མི་སྲིད། འདི་ལ་གཅེས་འཛིན་བྱས་པས་ཆགས་སྡང་གི་ལས་སྣ་ཚོགས་བསགས། དེ་ལས་འཇིག་རྟེན་གྱི་སྡུག་བསྔལ་ཐམས་ཅད་འབྱུང་བ
ཡིན་པས་འདི་ལ་གཅེས་འཛིན་དོར་དགོས། བདག་གི་བ་ལུས་ནི། སྟོན་བསགས་བཟང་པོའི་འབྲས་བུ་དང་། དམ་པའི་ཆོས་ལ་བཀོལ་ན་ཐར་པའི་རྟེན་བཟང་ཡིན་པས་ཟས་གོས་སྨན
སོགས་ཀྱིས་གཅེས་སྤྲས་བྱ་བ་ཤིན་ཏུ་གལ་ཆེ་ཞིང་། འོན་ཀྱང་ལུས་འདི་སེམས་ཅན་ལ་བཏང་བ་ཡིན་པས་བདག་འཛིན་བྱ་མི་རིགས་ཏེ། ཞི་བ་ལྷས། །བདག་གིས་སེམས་ཅན་ཐམས་ཅད་
ལ༑ །ལུས་འདི་ཅི་བདེར་བྱིན་ཟིན་གྱིས། །བརྡེག་སོགས་ཅི་དགར་བྱེད་ལ་རག །འདི་ཡི་ཁ་ཏས་ཅི་ཞིག་བྱ། གསུངས་པ་ལྟ་བུའོ། བློ་སྦྱོང་སློམ་པ་པོས་ལམ་ཁྱེར་ནི། །སྤྱོད་བཅུད་སྲིག
པས་གང་བའི་ཚེ། །རྐྱེན་ངན་བྱང་ཆུབ་ལམ་དུ་བསྒྱུར། ཞེས་པས་ཕྱི་སྣོད་འཇིག་རྟེན་གྱི་དཔལ་འབྱོར་ལ་འབྱུང་བཞིས་གནོད་འཚེ་དང་། མིས་བཟོས་པའི་དུག་རྫས་སོགས་ལ་བརྟེན་ནས

༄༅། །ཉམས་རྒྱུད་དུ་འགྲོ་བ་དང་། ནང་བཅུད་སེམས་ཅན་རྣམས་ཀྱི་དུག་ལྔ་སྟོབས་བདོ་བས་མི་དགེ་བ་སྡིག་པའི་ལས་སྤྱོད་པས་ལུས་ངག་ཡིད་གསུམ་གང་བའི་ཚེ། དེ་དག་ལ་བརྟེན་ནས་རང་ཐོག་ལ་རྐྱེན་ངན་པ་ཇི་ལྟར་བྱུང་ཡང་ལེ་ལེན་ངན་པ་མི་བསགས་པར། དཔེར་ན། རྗེ་བཙུན་མི་ལ་རས་པ་ཡུམ་སྲས་ལ། ཉེ་བས་སྡུག་ཚད་མེད་པ་བཏང་བས་ཚེ་གཅིག་དུ་སངས་རྒྱས་པའི་རྐྱེན་བཟང་པོ་བྱུང་བ་བཞིན་དུ་རང་ལ་སྡུག་བསྔལ་གྱི་རྐྱེན་ངན་པ་ཅི་ལྟར་ཐོག་ཏུ་བབས་ཀྱང་། དེ་རྣམས་བྱང་ཆུབ་ཀྱི་ལམ་དུ་བསྒྱུར་བར་བྱ་དགོས་ཤིང་དེ་ལ། །ལེ་ལན་ཐམས་ཅད་གཅིག་ཏུ་བདའ། ཞེས་པས་རང་གི་ལུས་ལ་ན་ཚ། སེམས་ཀྱི་སྡུག་བསྔལ། མི་ཁ་བསྒྱུར་འདེབས། དགྲ་རྒོད་ཁ་མཐུ། རྐུ་འཕྲོག་བཅོམ་བརྡུངས་སོགས་རང་དང་རང་གི་ཕྱོགས་ལ་མི་འདོད་པ་ཅི་བྱུང་ཡང་། གཟུགས་ཅན་གྱི་དགྲ་འམ་གཟུགས་མེད་ཀྱི་གདོན་བགེགས་འདི་ལྟ་བུས་བྱས་བྱུང་བསམ་པས། མོ་དང་རྩིས་ཚུན་ཆད་ཀྱིས་ཁག་ངན་ཕོ་ཚོའི་ཐོག་ཏུ་མི་འགེལ་བར། རང་རྒྱུད་ཀྱི་བདག་འཛིན་མ་རིག་པའི་སེམས་འདིས། བདག་གཞན་བར་མའི་འགྲོ་བ་རིས་སུ་བཅད་ནས་སྡིག་པ་མི་དགེ་བའི་ལས་སྣ་ཚོགས་བསགས་པ་ལ་བརྟེན་ནས།

དུག་ཐོས་ན་འཆི་བ་བཞིན་དུ་འཁོར་བ་ཐོག་མ་མེད་པ་ནས་སྡུག་བསྔལ་འདི་ལྟ་བུ་ཁོན་ལ་སྦྱོར་བར་བྱས་སོ་སྙམ་སྟེ། ལེ་ལན་ཐམས་ཅད་ཕུང་ཀྲོལ་བདག་འཛིན་འདི་གཅིག་པུའི་ཐོག་ཏུ་བདའ་ཞིང་ང་བདག་འཛིན་འདུལ་བའི་ཐབས་ལ། སངས་རྒྱས་ཀྱི་བཀའ་དང་བསྟན་བཅོས་ལུང་རིགས་གསུང་གི་སྣང་བ་ལ་ཐོས་བསམ་མམ། ཡང་ན་གསུང་རབ་རྣམས་ལ་སློང་ནས་དད་པ་དང་ཡིད་ཆེས་ཀྱིས། ཞི་བ་ལྷས། འཇིག་རྟེན་དག་ན་འཚེ་བ་གང་ཡོད་དང་། །འཇིགས་དང་སྡུག་བསྔལ་ཇི་སྙེད་ཡོད་གྱུར་པ། །དེ་ཀུན་བདག་ཏུ་འཛིན་པ་ལས་བྱུང་ན། །འདྲེ་ཆེན་དེས་ཀོ་བདག་ལ་ཅི་ཞིག་བྱ། ཞེས་སོགས་དང་། གཞན་ཡང་སྐྱབས་གནས་བླ་མ་དཀོན་མཆོག་ལ་རམ་དའ་སྦྲན་ནས་བདག་མེད་གནས་ལུགས་རྟོགས་པའི་གསོལ་འདེབས་གང་ཤེས་ལ་བརྩོན་པར་བྱ། མདོར་ན། ཐེག་པ་ཆེན་པོའི་རིགས་སད། བྱང་ཆུབ་མཆོག་ཏུ་སེམས་བསྐྱེད་ནས་བླ་མེད་བྱང་ཆུབ་ཐོབ་པའི་ཐབས་སུ་བསྟེན་བྱ་ལམ་གྱི་སྙིང་པོ་བསམ་སྦྱོར་གཉིས་ཀས་བདག་གཞན་བརྗེ་བ་ཡིན་པས། དུས་དང་སྤྱོད་ལམ་ཀུན་ཏུ་ལག་ལེན་ལ་ཅི་ཐེབས་བྱ་རྒྱུ་གལ་ཆེ་སྟེ། སངས་རྒྱས་ཀྱིས། དང་པོ་བྱང་ཆུབ་མཆོག་ཏུ་ཐུགས་བསྐྱེད་པའི་ཚུལ་ཡང་། ཐོག་མར་སོ་སྐྱེའི་

༄༅། །སྐབས་སུ། གཞན་གྱི་མགོ་བོའི་སྡུག་བསྔལ་རང་ལ་ལེན་པའི་སྙིང་རྗེའི་ཐུགས་བསྐྱེད་པའི་ས་བོན་ཙུང་ཟད་ལ་བརྟེན་ནས་སྐུ་སྐྱེ་མང་པོར་གོམས་ནས་སངས་རྒྱས་པའི་སྐབས་སུ། དམ་པའི་ཆོས་ཀྱི་འཁོར་ལོ་བསྐོར་ནས་གདུལ་བྱ་སེམས་ཅན་མང་པོའི་སྡུག་བསྔལ་བསལ་ནས་ཐར་པའི་ལམ་ནས་འདྲེན་པར་མཛད་པ་དང་། དེ་བཞིན་མི་ལ་རས་པ་སོགས་ཀྱིས་གང་མཛད་པ་ཐམས་ཅད་བདག་གཞན་མཉམ་བརྗེའི་བྱང་ཆུབ་ཀྱི་སྤྱོད་པ་མཐར་ཕྱིན་པས་ཡིན། བདག་གཞན་བརྗེ་ཞེས་པའང་། དཔེར་ན། གཞན་གྱི་ཆམ་རིམས་རང་ལ་འགོས་བཅུག་ནས། གློ་ལུ་བ། ཧབ་སྦྲིད་རྒྱག་པ་སོགས་སྡུག་ལ་གཏད་པ་ཙམ་ལ་གོ་མི་རུང་ཞིང་དེས་གཞན་ལ་ཕན་པ་གང་ཡང་མེད། གལ་ཏེ་ཁོའི་ན་ཚ་རང་ལ་ལེན་ཐུབ་ན་དེ་དགོས་པ་ཡིན་ཏེ། རྒྱལ་སྲས་ཐོགས་མེད་ཀྱིས། སྤྲང་པོའི་ལུས་ནས་གོས་རྩབ་རྩལ་ཤིག་སློས་གང་བ་དེ་སྐྱུགས་བྲོ་མེད་པར་ཁོང་གིས་བཞེས། ཁོང་གི་ན་བཟའ་ཐེར་ཕྱུག་དེ་ལ་གཡོགས་མཛད་པ་ལྟ་བུ། ཁོང་ནང་བཞིན་ལག་ཏུ་ལེན་ཐུབ་པའི་སྙིང་རྗེའི་སྟོབས་ཡོད་ན་ཁོང་དང་། བླ་མ་བྱམས་པའི་རྣལ་འབྱོར་པ་དང་། རྗེ་བཙུན་མི་ལས་དུག་བཞེས་པ་ལྟ་བུ་དགོས་ཀྱང་། བདག་ལྟ་བུ་རང་དོན་གཅེས་

འཛིན་གྱི་ཁོལ་པོར་གྱུར་པས་ཤིན་ཏུ་དཀའ་བའི་བྱ་བ་ཡིན་རུང་སྐྱེ་བ་དང་ཚེ་རབས་ཐམས་ཅད་དུ་དེ་ལྟར་ནུས་པའི་སྨོན་ལམ་འདེབས་པ་དང་། དབུགས་ཀྱི་རྟ་ལ་བསྐྱོན་པའི་གཏོང་ལེན་དང་། འབྲས་བུ་ལམ་བྱེད་རྡོ་རྗེ་ཐེག་པའི་ཆོས་དང་མཇལ་བའི་བསྐལ་པ་བཟང་པོའི་སྐབས་འདིར། རིམ་གཉིས་ཀྱི་ལམ་ནས་འོད་ཟེར་སྤྲོ་བསྡུས་སྣོད་བཅུད་དག་པར་སྦྱོང་བ་དང་། ལུས་ཀྱི་སྡུག་བསྔལ་ཅན་ལ་སྨན་དང་ཟས་གོས་ནོར་རྫས། སེམས་ཀྱི་སྡུག་བསྔལ་ཅན་ལ་ཕན་པའི་ཐབས་སོགས་ལ་རང་གི་ནོར་རྫས་དང་། ལུས་ངག་སེམས་ཀྱི་དཀའ་ངལ་ཁུར་དུ་ལེན་ཏེ་བདག་གཞན་བརྗེ་བའི་བྱང་ཆུབ་ཀྱི་སྤྱོད་པ་ལ་བསླབ་པར་བྱས་ནས། ཅི་བྱུང་བྱང་ཆུབ་ཀྱི་ལམ་ལ་བསྒྱུར་བའི་ཐབས་ལ་འབད་དོ། ཡང་། །ཀུན་ལ་བཀའ་དྲིན་ཆེ་བར་བསྒོམ། ཞེས་པས་གནས་སྐབས་དང་མཐར་ཐུག་གི་ཕན་བདེ་བསམ་པ་བྱང་ཆུབ་ཀྱི་སེམས། སྦྱོར་བ་ལམ་ཕ་རོལ་ཏུ་ཕྱིན་པ་དྲུག་དང་ཚད་མེད་བཞི། མཐར་ཐུག་རྫོགས་པའི་སངས་རྒྱས་ཀྱི་གོ་འཕང་སོགས་ལེགས་ཚོགས་མ་ལུས་པ་སེམས་ཅན་ལ་བརྟེན་ནས་འབྱུང་བ་ཡིན་པས་ན་ཀུན་ལ་རིས་ཆད་དུ་མ་སོང་བར་བཀའ་དྲིན་ཆེ་བར་བསྒོམ་པར་བྱ་སྟེ། རང་ལ་གནོད་པར་བྱེད་པའི་སེམས་ཅན་དགྲ་འདྲེ་ལན་ཆགས་

བཅུ་གསུམ་

༄༅། །ཀུན་ནི། བཟོད་པའི་ཕ་རོལ་ཏུ་ཕྱིན་པར་བྱེད་པའི་གྲོགས་བཀའ་དྲིན་ཅན་ཡིན་པས། ཁོའི་གནོད་སེམས་ཞི་ནས་རྒྱུད་ལ་ཡོད་པའི་ལས་ཉོན་སྡིག་སྒྲིབ་ཐམས་ཅད་དག་པའི་ཐབས་ལ་འབད། དེ་བཞིན་དུ་ལུས་ལ་ན་ཚ། སེམས་ལ་སྡུག་བསྔལ། དྲིན་ལན་ལོག་འཇལ། གྲོགས་ཀྱིས་བསླུ་བྲིད་སོགས་མི་འདོད་པ་དུ་མ་ཐོག་ཏུ་གང་བབ་ཡང་ལས་ཉོན་སྦྱོང་བའི་ཕྱུགས་མ། འཁོར་བའི་མཚང་འཕུད། དགེ་བའི་བསྐུལ་མ་ཡིན་པར་བསམ་སྟེ་གཏོང་ལེན་སོགས་དགེ་བའི་ཕྱོགས་སུ་བསྒྱུར་ནས་སེམས་སྐྱིད་ཡངས་སུ་བཏང་། རང་ལ་ལུས་ངག་ཡིད་ཀྱི་སྒོ་ནས་ཟས་གོས་སོགས་ཕན་པ་དང་བདེ་བའི་ཐབས་བྱེད་པའི་སེམས་ཅན་མཆོག་དམན་ཀུན་ལ་བཀའ་དྲིན་ཆེ་བར་བསམ་ནས་གཏོང་ལེན་སོགས་དྲིན་ལན་དགེ་བས་འཇལ། བར་མའི་སེམས་ཅན་སོགས་འགྲོ་བ་ཀུན་ལ། ཞི་བ་ལྷའི་གསུངས་བཞིན། བདག་གཞན་མཉམ་པ། བདག་བས་གཞན་གཅེས། བདག་གཞན་བརྗེ་བ་སོགས་བསྒོམ་པ་ལ་བསླབ་སྟེ་དངོས་སུ་ཕན་འདོགས་ཅི་ནུས་དང་། བརྒྱུད་ནས་སྨོན་འཇུག་གིས་བློ་སྦྱངས་ནས། བདག་ལ་བཟང་ངན་ལས་ཀྱིས་གང་འབྲེལ་བ་ཐམས་ཅད་བྱང་ཆུབ་ཐོབ་པའི་སྨོན་ལམ་བྱེད་པ་སོགས་ཀུན་རྫོབ་བྱང་

ཆུབ་སེམས་ལ་བརྟེན་ནས་ལུས་སེམས་ཀྱི་སྡུག་བསྔལ་ཐམས་ཅད་ཞི་བའི་ཐབས་ལ་འབད། དོན་དམ་བྱང་ཆུབ་སེམས་ལ་བརྟེན་ནས་སྡུག་བསྔལ་སྟོང་ཉིད་ཀྱི་ངང་དུ་གཅོད་པའི་ཐབས་ནི། །འཁྲུལ་སྣང་སྒྱུ་བཞིན་ལྟ་བ་ཡི། །སྟོང་ཉིད་སྲུང་བ་བླ་ན་མེད། ཅེས་པས་རང་གི་ལུས་སེམས་ལ་སྡུག་བསྔལ་གྱི་རིགས་མི་འདོད་པ་ཅི་བྱུང་ཡང་རང་སེམས་འཁྲུལ་པའི་དབང་གིས་སྣང་བ་མ་གཏོགས་ཕྱི་ནང་གི་ཆོས་ཐམས་ཅད་དོན་དུ་གྲུབ་མ་མྱོང་བ་རྨི་ལམ་ལྟར་ཐག་བཅད། འཁྲུལ་མཁན་སེམས་ལ་བལྟས་པས། སེམས་ཉིད་ངོ་བོ་སྟོང་པ་ཆོས་སྐུ། བེམ་སྟོང་ལྟར་མ་ཡིན་པར་རང་བཞིན་གསལ་བ་ལོངས་སྐུ། འཁོར་འདས་སྣ་ཚོགས་སུ་སྣང་བ་སྤྲུལ་སྐུ། དེ་གསུམ་གཉུག་མའི་དབྱིངས་སུ་གཟོད་ནས་དབྱེར་མེད་ངོ་བོ་ཉིད་ཀྱི་སྐུ་བཞིར་ངོ་སྤྲོད་ཅིང་ལྟ་བ་དེ་ཡི་ངང་དུ་མ་ཡེངས་པར་འཇོག་པ་ནི། མཐའ་བྲལ་ཟབ་མོ་སྟོང་པ་ཉིད་ཀྱི་སྲུང་བ། སྡུག་བསྔལ་འཁྲུལ་སྣང་སྒྱུ་བཞིའི་ཀློང་དུ་གྲོལ་བའི་བྱེད་པའི་ཐབས་བླ་ན་མེད་པ་ཡིན་ནོ། དེ་ཡང་རྒྱུན་དུ་གལ་ཆེ་བའི་སྦྱོར་བའམ་ལག་ཏུ་ལེན་བྱ་ནི། །སྦྱོར་བ་བཞི་ལྡན་ཐབས་ཀྱི་མཆོག །ཅེས་པས་ཚོགས་བསགས་པའི་སྦྱོར་བ། སྡིག་པ་བཤགས་པའི་སྦྱོར་བ། ལྷ་འདྲེ་ལ་གཏོར་མ་སྦྱིན་པའི་སྦྱོར་བ།

༄༅། །ཆོས་སྐྱོང་ལ་མཆོད་གཏོར་འབུལ་བའི་སྦྱོར་བ་བཞི་དང་ལྡན་པ་ནི་བྱང་ཆུབ་བསྒྲུབ་པའི་ལམ་གྱི་འགལ་རྐྱེན་ཐམས་ཅད་མྱུར་དུ་ཞི་ཞིང་ཉམས་རྟོགས་མཐར་ཕྱིན་པའི་ཐབས་ཀྱི་མཆོག་ཡིན་ཅིང་། དང་པོ་ནི། ཧེ་ལོ་པས། བུ་སྣང་བ་རྟེན་ཅིང་འབྲེལ་འབྱུང་འདི། །དོན་སྐྱེ་བ་མེད་པར་མ་རྟོགས་བར། །ཚོགས་གཉིས་ཤིང་རྟའི་འཕང་ལོ་ལ། །འབྲལ་བར་མ་བྱེད་ན་རོ་པ། གསུངས་པ་བཞིན། དམིགས་བཅས་བསོད་ནམས་ཀྱི་ཚོགས་རྫོགས་པའི་ཆེད་དུ། ཐེག་པའི་གསུམ་གྱི་སྡོམ་པ་དམ་ཚིག་གང་ནུས་བསྲུང་། ཆོས་མཛད་བཟང་པོ་ཞིག་གིས། བསླབ་པ་སྣ་རེ་རེ་ལའང་ཡིད་བཞིན་ནོར་བུ་གཙུག་ཏུ་ཁུར་བ་ལྟར་འགངས་ཆེན་དང་དད་གུས་བྱེད་ནས་མ་ཞོར་བ་དགོས་གསུང་གི་འདུག་པ་བསླབ་བྱ་ལེགས་པོར་སློམ། དེ་བཞིན་སྐྱ་གསུང་ཐུགས་རྟེན་གསར་བཞེངས། རྙིང་པ་ཉམས་གསོ། དེ་རྣམས་ཀྱིས་གཙོས་ཡར་བླ་མ་དཀོན་མཆོག་ལ་ཡན་ལག་བདུན་པའི་སྒོ་ནས་ཕྱག་མཆོད་བསྙེན་བཀུར། མར་ངན་སོང་ལ་སྦྱིན་གཏོང་། ནད་པ་ལ་སྨན་དང་། སྨན་ཁང་འཛུགས་བསྐྲུན་སོགས་མདོར་ན་ཚོགས་གང་ནུས་བསགས་ཏེ་བསྔོ་བ་དང་སྨོན་ལམ་རྒྱ་ཆེས་རྒྱས་གདབ་པར་བྱ། བོད་ཀྱི་ཆོས་ལ་ཞུགས་པའི་སྐྱེ་བོ་

ཕོ་མོ་སུ་ཡིན་ཀྱང་སོ་ཐར་སྡོམ་པ་ལས་དགེ་བསྙེན་སོགས་ཅི་རིགས་ནོས། བྱང་ཆུབ་སེམས་བསྐྱེད་ཐོབ། གསང་སྔགས་ཀྱི་དབང་ཆེན་དང་རྗེས་གནང་ལན་གཅིག་ཙམ་ཐོབ་མ་མྱོང་བ་མེད་པས༑ དགེ་འདུན་པ་ཁོ་ནའི་བསྲུང་བྱ་ལྟ་བུ་མ་ཡིན་པར་སེར་སྐྱ་ཡོངས་ནས་སྲུང་ས་བླང་ས་བྱེད་ནས་ཚོགས་ཆེན་རྫོགས་པའི་ཐབས་ལ་འབད་ནས་ཡུལ་ལ་ཆོས་ལྡན། མི་ལ་ཆོས་པ་ཞེས་པའི་མིང་དོན་མཐུན་དུ་འགྱུར་བའི་སྨོན་ལམ་ཚུན་བགྱིད་དོ། དམིགས་མེད་ཡེ་ཤེས་ཀྱི་ཚོགས་ལ། བློ་སྦྱོང་གི་དམིགས་རྣམ་དང་རིམ་གཉིས་ཀྱི་རྣམ་འབྱོར་སོགས་གང་ལ་བརྩོན་རུང་། སྦྱོར་བ་སེམས་བསྐྱེད། དངོས་གཞི་དགེ་བ་གང་བྱེད་འཁོར་གསུམ་དམིགས་མེད་ཀྱིས་རྒྱས་ཐེབས་པ། རྗེས་བསྔོ་བ་བཅས་དམ་པ་གསུམ་གྱིས་རྩིས་ཟིན་པས་བྱས་ཚད་ཚོགས་གཉིས་ཟུང་འབྲེལ་དུ་འགྲོ་ཞིང་། ཁྱད་པར་དུ་སེམས་ཉིད་གཉུག་མའི་གཤིས་ལུགས་གསལ་སྟོང་འཛིན་མེད་ཀྱི་ངང་དུ་འཇོག་པ་ནི་འབྲས་བུ་ཆོས་སྐུའི་ས་བོན་དོན་དམ་བྱང་ཆུབ་སེམས་ཀྱི་ཚོགས་ཆེན་རྫོགས་པའི་ཐབས་ཡིན་པར་བཞེད། གཉིས་པ་ནི། བདག་འཛིན་མ་རིག་འཁྲུལ་པའི་དབང་གིས་ཐོག་མ་མེད་པ་ནས་བསགས་པའི་སྡིག་པ་མི་དགེ་བ་ཇི་སྙེད་ཡོད་པ་དང་། ཁྱད་པར་དུ་ལུས་རྟེན་འདིར་

བཅོ་ལྔ་ 29

༄༅། །ལུས་ངག་ཡིད་གསུམ་གྱི་སྒོ་ནས་མི་དགེ་བ་བཅུ་དང་། ཁྱད་པར་ཕྱི་འདུལ་བ། ནང་ཐེག་པ་ཆེན་པོའི་བསླབ་བྱ། གསང་བ་རྡོ་རྗེ་ཐེག་པའི་དམ་ཚིག་དང་
འགལ་བ་རང་གིས་ཚོར་བ་དང་མ་ཚོར་བ་དང་། ལེ་ལོ་ཆེ་བ་དང་། བག་མེད་པ་དང་། ཉོན་མོང་མང་ཞིང་ཤུགས་དྲག་པ་དང་། བརྗེད་ངས་ཀྱི་དབང་དུ་གྱུར་པས་ཉེས་ལྟུང་ཆར་ཆེན་བཞིན་
འབེབས་པ་ཆོས་ཉིད་བདག་ལྟ་བུ་རྣམས་ལ། སྐྱབས་ཡུལ་སོགས་རྟེན་གྱི་སྟོབས་དང་། ཉེས་པ་མཐོལ་ཞིང་སུན་འབྱིན་པའི་སྟོབས་དང་། དགེ་བའི་ལས་སོགས་གཉེན་པོ་ཀུན་ཏུ་སྤྱོད་པའི་
སྟོབས་དང་། སླར་བསྡོམས་པའི་སྟོབས་ཏེ། སྟོབས་བཞིའི་སྒོ་ནས་ནུས་ན་ཉི་མ་རེ་རེ་བཞིན་ལྟུང་བཤགས་ལན་གསུམ། རྡོར་སེམས་ཡིག་གེ་བརྒྱ་པ། བརྒྱ་རྩས་མཆོན་ཁ་དོན་བཟླས་
བརྗོད་སོགས་སྡིག་སྒྲིབ་འདག་པའི་ཐབས་ལ་འབད་ནས་ཡང་ཡང་བཤགས་སྡོམ་བྱེད་ཐུབ་ན་མྱུར་དུ་སྒྲིབ་བྱང་ཚོགས་ཆེན་རྫོགས་པ་ཡིན་ཞེས་གསུངས་སོ། གསུམ་པ་ནི། རྗེ་བཙུན་མི་ལ་རས་
པས༑ །ལར་ཐམས་ཅད་སེམས་སུ་མ་ཤེས་ན། །རྣམ་རྟོག་གི་འདྲི་ལ་ཟད་པ་མེད། གསུངས་པ་བཞིན་ཕན་གནོད་ཀྱི་ལྷ་འདྲེར་སྣང་བ་ཐམས་ཅད་ཀྱང་། བདག་འཛིན་མ་རིག་པའི་རང

30

གཟུགས༑ སེམས་སྐྱེ་མེད་ཀྱི་ཆོ་འཕྲུལ་ཡིན་ཀྱང་། ཇི་སྲིད་གཉིས་འཛིན་གྱི་རྟོག་པ་མ་ཞིག་བར་དུ་ཕན་གནོད་བྱེད་པའི་ལྷ་འདྲེ་ཡོད་ངེས་པས། དེ་དག་ལ་གནོད་པའི་ལས་མི་བརྩམ་པར
བསངས་དང་། གཏོར་མ། གསུར་བསྔོ། ཁྱད་པར་དུ་མི་ལས། །ཕུང་པོ་གཟན་དུ་བསྒྱུར་བ་འདི། །བདག་འཛིན་འདུལ་བའི་ལམ་མཁན་ཡིན། གསུངས་པ་ལྟར། ཕུང་པོ་གཟན་
བསྒྱུར་ཞེས་རང་གི་ལུས་ཅི་འདོད་ཀྱི་ཟས་སུ་བསྒྱུར་ནས་ལུས་སྦྱིན་གཏོང་བ་དང་། སྙིང་རྗེའི་གཏོང་ལེན་སོགས་མདོར་ན། ལྷ་འདྲི་རྣམས་བདེ་བ་དང་མགུ་བའི་ཐབས་ལ་འབད་ཅིང་། ཁྱད་
པར་ནག་ཕྱོགས་ཀྱི་ལྷ་དང་། བདུད་བགེགས་འདྲེ་གདོན་རྣམས་ནི། ལས་ངན་གྱི་དབང་གིས་དེ་དག་ཏུ་སྐྱེས་ཏེ་གཞན་ལ་འཚེ་བར་བྱེད་པ་ཡིན་པས་ཕོ་ཚོའི་སྡིག་སྒྲིབ་ཐམས་ཅད་ཡོངས་སུ་ཞི་
ནས་བྱང་ཆུབ་མཆོག་ལ་འགོད་པའི་བསྔོ་བ་དང་སྨོན་ལམ་གདབ། བཞི་པ་ནི། སྟོན་པ་ཐུབ་པའི་དབང་པོ། རྒྱལ་དབང་པདྨ་ཀཱ་ར། བཞད་པ་རྡོ་རྗེ་སོགས་སྟོན་བྱོན་སྐྱེས་མཆོག་རྣམས་ཀྱིས
དམ་ལ་བཞག་ཅིང་བསྟན་པ་གཉེན་པོ་བསྲུང་ཞིང་ཕྲིན་ལས་བསྒྲུབ་པར་ཁས་བླངས་པའི་ཆོས་སྐྱོང་ལྷམ་དྲལ་རྣམས་ལ་མཆོད་གཏོར་འབུལ་ཞིང་འདོད་དོན་ཕྲིན་ལས་བཅོལ། ཁྱད་པར་ཡེ་ཤེས

༄༅། །སྤྱན་ལྡན་རྣམས་ལ། བདག་མེད་གནས་ལུགས་རྟོགས་ཤིང་བློ་སྦྱོང་སྒོམ་པ་མཐར་ཕྱིན་ནས་འགྲོ་དོན་རྒྱ་ཆེན་འགྲུབ་པའི་ལས་བཙོལ། འོ་ན། དྲག་པོས་དགྲ་བགེགས་སྒྲོལ་བའི་ལས་བཙོལ་དོན་གང་ཡིན་ཞེ་ན། བསྒྲལ་བྱའི་རྣམ་ཤེས་བདེ་ཆེན་དུ་སྤོར་བས་ལས་ངན་གྱི་རྒྱུན་བཅད་ནས་སངས་རྒྱས་ཀྱི་ས་ལ་སྐད་ཅིག་ཏུ་འདྲེན་པའི་ཐབས་སྙིང་རྗེས་བཟུང་དགོས་ཕྱིར་ཞེ་སྡང་གིས་བསད་པ་མ་ཡིན་པས་བྱང་ཆུབ་སེམས་ཀྱིས་བློ་སྦྱོང་བ་ལ་ནམ་ཡང་འགལ་བ་མེད་སྙམ། གསང་སྔགས་ཀྱི་རྣལ་འབྱོར་པ་ནུས་པ་ཐོབ་ན་ཞིང་བཅུ་བསྒྲལ་འདྲེན་མ་བགྱིས་ན་རྩ་ལྟུང་འབྱུང་བར་གསུངས་པས་ཞེས་སོ། དེས་རྐྱེན་ངན་ལམ་དུ་བྱེད་པའི་དངོས་གཞི་བསྟན་ནས། ཐུན་མཚམས་ལ་བློ་བུར་དུ་བཟང་ངན་ཅི་བྱུང་ཡང་བསྒོམ་ལ་སྦྱོར་བའི་ཕྱིར། །འཕྲལ་ལ་གང་ཐུག་བསྒོམ་དུ་སྦྱར། ཞེས་པས་བློ་བུར་དུ་གཞན་གྱིས་རང་ངམ་རང་གི་ཕྱོགས་ལ་བརྡུང་བརྡེག་གམ་བརྙས་སྨོད་བྱེད་པ། གཟུགས་པོར་བརྡབས་ཆག་བྱུང་བ། ནོར་རྫས་འཕྲོག་བཅོམ། གཏམ་ངན་ཐོས་པ། བློ་བུར་ལུས་ལ་ན་ཚ་ཕོག་པ། གནོད་པ་དང་འཁོན་དྲན་པ་སོགས་སེམས་ལ་ཟུག་རྔུ་དྲག་པོ། ཉོན་མོངས་དུག་ལྔ་གང་རུང་དྲག་པོ་སྐྱེས་པ། རྨིས་

ལྟས་ངན་པ། འདྲེ་གདོན་མཐོང་སྣང་སོགས་འཕྲུལ་ལ་མི་འདོད་པ་གང་ལྟ་བུ་རང་ཐོག་ཏུ་བབས་པའམ་ཐུག་བྱུང་ཡང་། ལན་དུ་སྡུག་བསྔལ་དང་གནོད་སེམས་ཁོང་ཁྲོ་སོགས་མི་བྱེད་པར། ༈བླ་མ་དཀོན་མཆོག་ཐུགས་རྗེས། རྐྱེན་ངན་པ་ནམ་བྱུང་ཐམས་ཅད་བཟོད་པ་བསྒོམ་པ་སོགས་དགེ་བའི་ལམ་དུ་བསྒྱུར་བའི་བསྐུལ་མ་མཛད་པ་འམ། རང་གིས་གཞན་ལ་འདི་ལྟ་བུའི་གནོད་འཚེ་དུ་མ་བྱས་ཤིང་བསགས་པའི་ལེ་ལན་འཁོར་བ་ཡིན་ངེས། གང་ལྟར་ཡང་། མཁའ་ཁྱབ་ཀྱི་སེམས་ཅན་ཐམས་ཅད་ཀྱི་མི་འདོད་པའི་རྐྱེན་ངན་བར་ཆད་ཐམས་ཅད་བདག་གི་འདི་ཐོག་ཏུ་འདུས་ཤིང་འདིས་གོ་ཆོད་ནས། སེམས་ཅན་ཐམས་ཅད་བདེ་སྐྱིད་ཕུན་སུམ་ཚོགས་པ་ལ་གནས་པར་གྱུར་ཅིག་སྙམ་པ་སོགས་ཀྱིས། མ་བསམ་བཞིན་དུ་བློ་བུར་དུ་བྱུང་བའི་མི་འདོད་པ་ཐམས་ཅད་བློ་སྦྱོང་གི་བསྒོམ་ལ་སྦྱར་ཞིང་གཏོང་ལེན་བྱེད། ཡང་ན་འཕྲལ་དུ་སེམས་ལ་སྐྱིད་སྣང་བྱུང་བ། ལུས་ལ་ཟས་གོས་སྨན་སོགས་ཀྱིས་བློ་བུར་ཚོར་བ་བདེ་བ། གཞན་གྱིས་བསྟོད་བསྔགས་བརྗོད་པ། དད་གུས་དང་ནོར་རྫས་ཕུལ་པ། མིག་ལ་མི་རྟག་གི་ཚལ་དང་བྲོ་གར། རྣ་བར་གླུ་དང་སྒྲ་སྙན། སྣར་དྲི་ཞིམ་པ་སོགས་མདོར་ན་བློ་བུར་དུ་ཡིད་དགའ་བའི་རྐྱེན་

༄༅། །བཟང་པོ་ཕྱོགས་དུས་གང་ནས་འཕྲད་ཀྱང་། རྣ་བླ་མ་དཀོན་མཆོག་གི་བྱིན་བརླབས་ཡིན་སྙམ་སྟེ། དེ་རྣམས་ལ་ཡིད་ཀྱིས་མཆྭལ་དུ་འབུལ་བ་དང་། འདི་
དག་གིས་བཅིངས་ནས་ངརྒྱལ་དང་ཞེན་པས་བདག་གཅེས་འཛིན་གྱི་བསྐྱོན་མ་རམི་འགྱུར་བར་བྱའོ་བསམ་ཞིང་། འདིས་མཚོན་པའི་བདག་གི་བདེ་སྐྱིད་དང་ལེགས་ཚོགས་ཐམས་ཅད།
རིགས་དྲུག་གི་སེམས་ཅན་བདེ་དགས་ཡོངས་པ་རྣམས་ལ་སྦྱིན་ནོ་སྙམ་ནས་གཏོང་ལེན་གྱི་བསྒོམ་ལ་སྦྱར་བར་བྱའོ། མདོར་ན་གླང་ཐང་པས། རྐྱེན་ངན་བྱང་ཆུབ་ལམ་དུ་བསྒྱུར་བྱ་བ་རེ་
དོགས་གཉིས་འགགས་པ་ཡིན། དེ་མ་ཁེགས་བར་རྐྱེན་ངན་ལམ་དུ་ཁྱེར་མི་ནུས་གཏོང་ལེན་སོགས་སྦྱོང་བ་ནི་ཤིང་འཁྲུག་པོ་བསྲོང་བ་དང་འདྲ་གསུངས་སོ། དེ་ཡང་བདུན་ཕྲུག་དང་ཟླ་བ་རེ་
ཟུང་ལ་བློ་སྦྱོང་ཉམས་སུ་བླངས་པའི་ཁ་ཡོ་ཙམ་གྱིས་མི་ཕན་པར་ཚེ་གཅིག་ལ་ཉམས་སུ་ལེན་དགོས་པར་གསུངས་ཏེ། །མན་ངག་སྙིང་པོ་མདོར་བསྡུས་པ། །སྟོབས་ལྔ་དག་དང་སྦྱར་བར་བྱ།
ཞེས་པས་སངས་རྒྱས་ཀྱིས་གསུངས་པའི་དམ་པའི་ཆོས་ཀུན་གྱི་ཉམས་ལེན་གནད་དུ་དྲིལ་བའི་མན་ངག་སྙིང་པོ་མདོར་བསྡུས་པ་ནི་སྟོབས་ལྔ་པོ་འདི་དག་དང་སྦྱར་བར་བྱ་དགོས་པས། དང་

པོ་འཕེན་པའི་སྟོབས་ནི། གཞན་དོན་འབྱུང་བའི་སློ། བདག་འཛིན་འདུལ་བའི་གཉེན་པོ་བྱང་ཆུབ་ཀྱི་སེམས་ལ་བློ་སྦྱོང་བའི་གདམས་ངག་ཟབ་མོ་འདི། དུས་འདི་ནས་བཟུང་སྟེ་མ་ཤི་བར་དུ
ཉམས་ལེན་ལ་སྦྱར་ནས་ལག་ཏུ་ཅི་ལོན་བྱའོ་སྙམ་པའི་འདུན་པ་ཤུགས་དྲག་དང་མ་བྲལ་བར་བྱ། གཉིས་པ། གོམས་པའི་སྟོབས་ནི། ཇི་ལྟར་འཕེན་པ་བཏང་བ་ལྟར། གནས་གང་དུ་སོང་།
གྲོགས་སུ་དང་འགྲོགས། སྐྱིད་སྡུག་ཅི་ལྟར་གྱུར་ཀྱང་། རྐྱེན་ངན་དང་སྡིག་གྲོགས་སོགས་ཀྱིས་དབང་དུ་མི་བཏང་བར། བློ་སྦྱོང་ཆོས་ཀྱི་གནད་དོན། ལྟ་བ་ཟབ་མོ་རྟེན་འབྱུང་། སྒོམ་པ
མཆོག་གྱུར་བྱང་ཆུབ་ཀྱི་སེམས། སྤྱོད་པ་རླབས་ཆེན་ཕྱིན་དྲུག་སོགས་ལ་ཅི་ནུས་ཀྱིས་གོམས་པར་བྱེད་ནས་འབྲས་བུ་བླ་མེད་སངས་རྒྱས་ཀྱི་གོ་འཕང་ཐོབ་པར་བགྱིད་དོ་སྙམ་པ་དང་། བླ་མ
དཀོན་མཆོག་ལའང་དེ་བཞིན་འགྲུབ་པའི་མཐུན་འགྱུར་གསོལ་བ་འདེབས། གསུམ་པ་དཀར་པོ་ས་བོན་གྱི་སྟོབས་ནི། བྱང་ཆུབ་ཀྱི་སེམས་མ་སྐྱེས་པ་སྐྱེ། སྐྱེས་པ་མི་ཉམས་ཤིང་གོང་ནས
གོང་དུ་འཕེལ་བའི་ཆེད་དུ། ཐ་ན་སེམས་ཅན་ལ་ཟས་ཁམ་གཅིག་ཙམ་སྦྱིན་པའི་དགེ་རྩ་ཚུན་ཆད་ནས་བསགས་ཏེ། ལུས་ངག་ཡིད་གསུམ་ཚོགས་གཉིས་རྫོགས་པའི་ཐབས་སམ་ས་བོན་ལ

༄༅། །འབད་དོ། བཞི་པ་སྨུན་འབྱིན་པའི་སྟོབས་ནི། སེམས་ཅན་གཅིག་ཙམ་ལ་ཕན་པ་མི་བྱེད་སྙམ་པའི་ཡལ་བར་འདོར་བའི་བློ་དང་། དགེ་བ་བྱས་པ་རང་དོན་ཡིད་བྱེད་ཀྱི་བློ་བྱུང་ན། བྱང་ཆུབ་སེམས་ཀྱི་གཏན་བདེའི་ནོར་བུ་འདོར་བ་ཡིན་འདུག་སྙམ་ནས་འགྱོད་པ་དྲག་པོས་སྨུན་འབྱིན་པར་བྱ། ལྔ་པ་སྨོན་ལམ་གྱི་སྟོབས་ནི། རྟེན་གྱི་དྲུང་ངམ། དུས་ཀུན་ཏུ་སྨོན་ལམ་གདབ་པར་བྱ་སྟེ། །སྤྱིར་སེམས་ཅན་ཐམས་ཅད་བདག་ཁོ་ནས་སངས་རྒྱས་ཀྱི་ས་ལ་འདྲེན་ནུས་པར་གྱུར་ཅིག ཁྱད་པར་དུས་འདི་ནས་སངས་རྒྱས་མ་ཐོབ་ཀྱི་བར་དུ་བྱང་ཆུབ་ཀྱི་སེམས་རིན་པོ་ཆེ་རྣམ་པ་གཉིས་རྨི་ལམ་དུའང་མི་བརྗེད་ཅིང་གོང་ནས་གོང་དུ་འཕེལ་བར་ཤོག་ཅིག རྐྱེན་ངན་ཅི་བྱུང་ཡང་བྱང་ཆུབ་སེམས་ཀྱི་གྲོགས་སུ་ཁྱེར་ནུས་པར་གྱུར་ཅིག ཅེས་དང་། གཞན་ཡང་བཟང་པོ་སྤྱོད་པ་སོགས། མདོ་ལས་འབྱུང་བའི་བྱང་ཆུབ་སེམས་དཔའི་སྨོན་ལམ་རླབས་ཆེན་ལ་བརྩོན་པར་བྱ་ཞིང་ནམ་ཞིག་འཆི་བའི་ཚེ་ན། །ཐེག་ཆེན་འཕོ་བའི་གདམས་ངག་ནི། །སྟོབས་ལྔ་ཉིད་ཡིན་སྤྱོད་ལམ་གཅེས། ཞེས་པས། ཐེག་པ་ཆེན་པོའི་སྙིང་པོ་བློ་སྦྱོང་སྒོམ་པ་པོ་ཚེའི་དུས་བྱེད་པ་ན་འཕོ་བའི་གདམས་ངག་ཟབ་མོ་ནི། བསྟན་

སྟོབས་ལྔ་ཉིད་ཡིན་པས། དང་པོ་དཀར་པོ་ས་བོན་གྱི་སྟོབས་ནི། བློ་སྦྱོང་ཉམས་སུ་བླངས་པའི་གང་ཟག་འཆི་ནད་ཐེབས་པ་ན། རང་ལ་དབང་བའི་ནོར་རྫས་མང་ཉུང་ཅི་མཆིས་ཡར་མཆོད་པ། མར་སྦྱིན་གཏོང་སོགས་རང་གིས་གང་མོས་བཞིན་དགེ་བའི་རྩ་བར་བཏང་ནས་ཞེན་ཆགས་མེད་པར་བྱ་ཞིང་སྡོམ་པ་དམ་ཚིག་ཉམས་ཆག་ཐམས་ཅད་བཤགས་པར་བྱ། གཉིས་པ་སྨོན་ལམ་གྱི་སྟོབས་ནི། བདག་གི་ཕུང་པོའི་རོ་སྲེག་བ། དྲི་ཆོར་བ་ལུས་ཀྱི་རྡུལ་ཕྲ་རབ་གང་དུ་ཐིམ་པའི་སྣོད་བཅུད་ཐམས་ཅད་དག་པའི་ཞིང་གི་རྟེན་བརྟེན་པར་འགྱུར་བ་དང་། འདི་ནས་འཕོས་མ་ཐག་ཏུ་སྤྲུལ་པ་གྲངས་དང་ཚད་མེད་པས་སེམས་ཅན་གཅིག་ཙམ་ཡང་མ་ལུས་པའི་སྡུག་བསྔལ་དང་སྡུག་བསྔལ་གྱི་རྒྱུ་ཐམས་ཅད་བསལ། བདེ་བ་དང་བདེ་བའི་རྒྱུ་ཕུན་སུམ་ཚོགས་པ་ལ་བཀོད་ནས་གནས་སྐབས་ཕན་པ་དང་མཐར་ཐུག །ཆབས་ཅིག་སངས་རྒྱས་ཀྱི་གོ་འཕང་ལ་འགོད་ནུས་པར་ཤོག་ཅིག ཅེས་སོགས་སྨོན་ལམ་རླབས་ཆེན་གདབ། གསུམ་པ་སྨུན་འབྱིན་པའི་སྟོབས་ནི། བདག་འཛིན་མ་རིག་པའི་བློ་འདིས་སྐྱེ་རྒ་ན་འཆིའི་སྡུག་བསྔལ་འདི་ལྟ་བུ་གྲངས་མེད་པ། ཐོག་མེད་ནས་མྱོང་ཡང་རྨི་ལམ་ལྟར་དོན་དམ་པར་བདེན་པར་མ་གྲུབ་ཅིང་སེམས་ཉིད་འོད་གསལ་

༄༅། །ཆོས་སྐུ་ལ་འཆི་རྒྱུ་མེད། ད་ལྟ་ནའོ་འཆིའོ་སོགས་ཚོར་བ་ཅི་བྱུང་ཐམས་ཅད་བདག་འཛིན་གྱི་རང་གཟུགས་བསྟན་པ་ཡིན་པས་བརྣག་པར་བྱའོ་སྙམ་སྟེ་ཐག་བཅད་དོ། །བཞི་པ་འཕེན་པའི་སྟོབས་ནི། སྨོན་འགྲོའི་སྐབས་ལྟར་རང་གི་སྤྱི་བོར་རྩ་བའི་བླ་མ་དང་འཕགས་མཆོག་སྤྱན་རས་གཟིགས་གསལ་བཏབ་པ་ལ་གསོལ་བ་འདེབས་ཤིང་ཐུགས་ཡིད་བསྲེ། བདག་གིས་བརྡོ་དང་སྐྱེ་བ་ཐམས་ཅད་དུ། བླ་མ་དཀོན་མཆོག་ལ་ཡིད་ཕྲེད་ཤེས་ཀྱི་དད་པ་དང་། བྱང་ཆུབ་ཀྱི་སེམས་རྣམ་པ་གཉིས་དང་མ་བྲལ་བར་བྱའོ་བསམ་པ་གང་ནུས་བསྐྱེད། ལྔ་པ་གོམས་པའི་སྟོབས་ནི། འཆི་ཁ་ནད་ཀྱི་གཟུག་གཟེར་དང་གཉེན་གྲོགས་སོགས་ལ་ཞེན་ཆགས་སོགས་ཀྱི་ཚོར་བ་དྲག་པ་བྱུང་ཡང་དེའི་དབང་དུ་མ་ཤོར་བ། སྨོན་བྱམས་སྙིང་རྗེ་བྱང་ཆུབ་ཀྱི་སེམས་རྣམ་པ་གཉིས་བསྒོམས་ཤིང་། གོམས་པ་དེ་དག་གསལ་ཆེ་རུ་བཏབ་ནས་གཏོང་ལེན་གྱི་དམིགས་པ་དང་། ད་ལྟའི་བར་ཆོས་ཉིད་རང་ངོ་མ་ཤེས་འཁྲུལ་པ་མ་གཏོགས་དོན་དམ་གཉུག་མ་བདེ་གཤེགས་སྙིང་པོའི་ངོ་བོ་ལ་སྐྱེ་འཆི་མེད་དོ་སྙམ་ནས་དེ་ངོར་མཉམ་པར་གཞག་པ་བཅས་ནི། འཆི་བའི་དུས་སུ་དགོས་པ་བསམ་པའི་སྟོབས་ལྔ་དང་། དེ་ཚེ་སྦྱོར་བ་སྤྱོད་ལམ་ལེགས་

པའམ་གཅེས་པ་ནི། གཞོག་གཡས་པ་ས་ཕབ། ལག་གཡས་པ་འགྲམ་པར་གཏད་པ་སོགས། སངས་རྒྱས་གཟིམ་སྟབས་ལ་བསླབ་རྒྱུ་ཞིབ་པ་གཞན་ནས་ཤེས་པར་བྱའོ། སྨོན་ཚད་བློ་སྦྱོང་བསྒོམས་པ་འབྱོངས་པའམ་གོམས་པའི་ཚད་བསྟན་པ་ནི། །ཆོས་ཀུན་དགོངས་པ་གཅིག་ཏུ་འདུས། ཞེས་པས་བཅོམ་ལྡན་འདས་ཀྱིས། ཕྱི་སོ་ཐར། ནང་བྱང་སེམས། གསང་བ་སྔགས་སོགས་དམ་པའི་ཆོས་ཀྱི་འཁོར་ལོ་ཟབ་ཅིང་རྒྱ་ཆེ་བ་བསྐོར་བར་མཛད་པ་ཀུན་གྱི་དགོངས་པ་ནི། རང་རྒྱུད་ལ་ཡོད་པའི་ཉེས་པ་ཐམས་ཅད་ཀྱི་རྩ་བ་བདག་འཛིན་མ་རིག་པ་འདུལ་བའི་ཆེད་ཁོ་ན་འམ་གཅིག་ཏུ་འདུས་འདུག་པར་གོ་ནས། རང་རྒྱུད་ཇེ་ཐུལ་དུ་འགྲོ་ཞིང་། བྱམས་སྙིང་རྗེ་རྗེ་ཆེར་སོང་ན་བློ་སྦྱོང་འབྱོངས་པའི་རྟགས་དང་ཆོས་ཉམས་སུ་བླངས་པས་རང་རྒྱུད་ལ་ཕན་ཐོག་གམ་མ་ཐོག་ཚད་ལ་འཇལ་བའི་རྒྱུམ་ལྟ་བུ་ཡིན་པར་གསུངས། ཡང་། །དཔང་པོ་གཉིས་ཀྱི་གཙོ་བོ་བཟུང་། ཞེས་པས་རང་ཉིད་ཆོས་པ་བཟང་པོ་ཡིན་མིན་གྱི་དཔང་པོ་ལ་རང་གཞན་གཉིས་ཀྱི་ནང་ནས། རང་བློ་རང་ལ་ལྐོག་ཏུ་མ་གྱུར་པའི་ཕྱིར་རང་གཙོ་བོ་བཟུང་དགོས། གཞན་གྱིས་བདག་ལ་ཆོས་པ་བཟང་པོ་ཡིན་པའི་བསྟོད་པ་དང་། ཡང་ན་ངན་པ་ཡིན་པའི་སྨད་པ་

༄༅། །བཏང་རྒྱང་། བསྟོད་པས་ང་རྒྱལ་གྱི་བསྟོན་པ་མ་གཏོགས་རང་རྒྱུད་ལ་མི་ཕན། སྨད་པ་བཏང་ཡང་བདག་ངན་པར་བསྒྱུར་མི་ནུས། དེ་བས་དུས་རྒྱུན་དུ་རང་
གི་དབང་པོ་ལ་རང་བཞག་ནས་གནོང་ས་འགྱོད་མེད་པ་བྱུང་ན་བློ་སྦྱོང་འབྱོངས་པའི་རྟགས་ཡིན་པར་གསུངས། ཡང་། །ཡིད་བདེ་འབབ་ཞིག་རྒྱུན་དུ་བརྟེན། ཞེས་པས་རང་གི་ལུས་སེམས་
ཀྱི་ཐོག་ལ་རྐྱེན་ངན་སྡུག་བསྔལ་མི་འདོད་པ་ཅི་བྱུང་ཡང་མི་ལ་བུད་ཤིང་བསྣན་པ་ལྟར་རྐྱེན་ངན་ལམ་ཁྱེར་བྱང་ཆུབ་སེམས་རྣམ་པ་གཉིས་བསྒོམ་པས་ཚོག་གི་བསམ་ནས་གྲོགས་སུ་སོང་ཏེ་ཡིད་
བདེ་འབབ་ཞིག་ཉིན་མཚན་སྤྱོད་ལམ་རྒྱུན་དུ་བློ་སྦྱོང་སྒོམ་པས་བརྟེན་ཐུབ་ན་འབྱོངས་པའི་རྟགས་དང་། ཡང་། །ཡེངས་ཀྱང་ཐུབ་ན་འབྱོངས་པ་ཡིན། ཞེས་པས་རྒྱུན་དུ་དོན་བདུན་མ་
སོགས་བློ་སྦྱོང་གི་ཚིག་དོན་རྣམས་ལ་གཞར་སྦྱོང་བགྱིས་པ་གོམས་པའི་ཚད་ནི། ཆེད་དུ་དྲན་པས་མ་བཟུང་ཡེངས་སྟད་ཀྱང་བློ་ཐོག་ནས་ཤར་ཤར་འདོན་ནས་དོན་དྲན་ནུས་པ་དང་། འཆི་བ
ནམ་ཡོང་ཆ་མེད་པས་གློ་བུར་དུ་བྱུང་ཡང་བྱང་ཆུབ་སེམས་རྣམ་པ་གཉིས་ཉམས་སུ་ལེན་པ་འདི་འདུན་མ་བཟང་སླམ་ནས་མི་འཆོར་བ་སོགས། མདོར་ན་རྐྱེན་ངན་དྲག་པོ་ཅི་བྱུང་ཡང་དེས་དབང་

དུ་མི་ཤོར་བར་ཀུན་རྫོབ་དང་དོན་དམ་བྱང་ཆུབ་སེམས་ཀྱི་གཉེན་པོས་དེ་མ་ཐག་འཇོམས་ཐུབ་ན་བློ་སྦྱོང་འབྱོངས་པའི་རྟགས་ངོ་མཚར་ཆེ་བ་ཡིན་རུང་། འོན་ཀྱང་འདི་ཙམ་གྱིས་མི་ཕན་པར།
གོམས་པ་མཐར་ཕྱིན་པ་སངས་རྒྱས་ཀྱི་གོ་འཕང་མ་ཐོབ་བར་བསྒོམ་དགོས་པར་གསུངས། མདོར་ན་གཏོང་ལེན་གཉིས་པོ་བསྒོམས་པས་ལུས་དང་སེམས་ལ་སྡུག་བསྔལ་ཅི་བྱུང་ཡང་མི་དགའ
བ་མེད་པར་དགའ་བས་ཁྱབ་སྟེ་བློ་སྦྱོང་གི་གྲོགས་སུ་འགྲོ་ཡིན་འདུག་ན་འབྱོངས་པའི་ཚད་ཡིན་གསུངས། ༈ སྐབས་འདིར་བཤེས་གཉེན་གཞན་གྱིས། །བྱང་བའི་ཚད་ནི་ལོག་པ་ཡིན། །
འབྱོངས་རྟགས་ཆེན་པོ་ལྔ་ལྡན་ཡིན། ཞེས་ཚིགས་བཅད་གཉིས་བསྣན་པའི་དོན་གསུངས་པ་ནི། གཞན་གཅེས་འཛིན་ལ་ཤིན་ཏུ་གོམས་པའི་ཚད་ནི། རང་གཅེས་འཛིན་ལས་བློ་ལོག་ནས་ཁེ
དང་རྒྱལ་ཁ་གཞན་ལ་འབུལ་བ་དང་། ཆེན་པོ་ལྔ་ནི། ཐེག་པ་ཆེན་པོའི་ཆོས་ཀྱིས་ཡིད་འཕྲོག་ནས་དད་པས་སློབ་ཅིང་བྱང་ཆུབ་སེམས་ལ་ཐུགས་དམ་གྱི་མཐིལ་བྱེད་པ་སེམས་དཔར་འམ་བློ་
གྲོས་ཆེན་པོ། ཉུང་མཐའ་ཕམ་ལྷག་ཙམ་མམ། ཉེས་ལྟུང་ཕྲ་རགས་ཐམས་ཅད་ལ་ཤིན་ཏུ་འཛེམས་ཤིང་། ཡར་མར་གྱི་གསོ་སྦྱོང་དང་། ཆོས་གོས་ལྷུང་བཟེད་སོགས་འབྲལ་སྤྱངས་ཀྱི

ཅེ་ར་གཅིག

༄༅། །རིགས་འཆང་བ། ཤ་ཆང་དང་དཀྲུང་བཅད་སོགས་འདུལ་བའི་ལག་ལེན་ཚུལ་བཞིན་བྱེད་པ་ནི་འདུལ་བ་འཛིན་པའི་མཁན་པོ་ཆེན་པོ། ཉོན་མོངས་འདུལ་བ་ལ་དཀའ་སྤྱད་ནུས་པས་བཀའ་ཐུབ་པ་ཆེན་པོ། ཆོས་སྤྱོད་བཅུ་དང་མི་འབྲལ་བས་དགེ་སྦྱོང་ཆེན་པོ། སྟོང་ཉིད་སྙིང་རྗེའི་ཉམས་ལེན་ལ་མི་འབྲལ་བས་རྣལ་འབྱོར་པ་ཆེན་པོ་བཅས་ཡིན་པར་གསུངས་པ་ནི། སྙིགས་མའི་སྐབས་འདིར་ཡུལ་དུས་གྲོགས་ཀྱི་དབང་གིས་ཚུལ་བཞིན་ལག་ལེན་བསྲུང་དཀའ་ནའང་བསླབ་བྱ་གལ་ཆེ་བར་འདུག བློ་སྦྱོང་སྒོམ་པ་པོའི་བསྲུང་བྱའི་དམ་ཚིག་བཅུ་དྲུག་ནི། དང་པོ། །སྤྱི་དོན་གསུམ་ལ་རྟག་ཏུ་བསླབ། གསུངས་ཏེ། དགོན་མཆོག་ལ་སྐྱབས་སུ་སོང་ནས་ལམ་བསླབ་པ་གསུམ་ལ་སློབ་པ་ནི་སྤྱི་ཡི་དོན་ཡིན་པས་བློ་སྦྱོང་སྒོམ་མཁན་ནས་ཀྱང་ཡལ་བར་མི་དོར་བར། བློ་སྦྱོང་ཁས་བླངས་དང་མ་འགལ་བ། བློ་སྦྱོང་ཐོ་ཅོར་མ་ཤོར་བ། བློ་སྦྱོང་ཕྱོགས་རིས་མ་ཤོར་བ་གསུམ་ལ་རྟག་ཏུ་བསླབ་དགོས་ཏེ། དང་པོ། ཐེག་པ་གསུམ་གྱི་བསླབ་བྱ་ཆེ་ཆུང་རང་གིས་གང་ཁས་བླངས་པ་དྲན་ཤེས་བག་ཡོད་ཀྱིས་ཉེས་ལྟུང་གིས་མ་གོས་པ་དང་། གལ་ཏེ་བྱུང་ན། དེ་མ་ཐག་བཤགས་སྦྱོང་ལ་འབད། གཉིས་པ།

བདག་གཅིག་འཛིན་མེད་པ་གཞན་ལ་ངོམས་པའི་དོན་དུ། རྟེན་གསུམ་དང་སྡོད་ས་ཐལ་རྡུལ་གྱིས་གཡོགས། ཟས་གོས་སོགས་ཛར་ཛོར་གང་དྲན་ལ་སྤྱོད་པ་འམ། གཉན་སར་ཉལ་བ་དང་ཤིང་གཉན་གཅོད་པ། ལྷ་རྟེན་བཤིགས་པ་དང་འགོ་བའི་ནད་ཡོད་སར་འགྲོ་བ་སོགས་ཐོ་ཅོའི་སྤྱོད་པ་མི་བྱེད་པར། དགེ་བཤེས་འབྲོམ་སྟོན་པའི་བཀའ་སློལ་བཞིན་དུ། ཕྱི་གཙང་ནང་གཙང་རྗེ་བོ་བཀའ་གདམས་པའི་རྣམ་ཐར་བཞིན་བྱ་དགོས་གསུངས། དེས་ན་གྲོང་ཁྱེར་སྐྱིད་པའི་འབྱུང་གནས་བྱ་བའང་བློ་སྦྱོང་སྒོམ་པའི་རྣལ་འབྱོར་པའི་ལུས་སེམས་གཙང་སེང་ངེ་བ་ལ་ཟེར་བ་ཡིན་གསུངས། གསུམ་པ། སེམས་ཅན་འགའ་རེའི་དོན་བྱེད་ལ་འགའ་རེའི་དོན་མི་བྱེད་པ་དང་། མི་ཆེ་བ་གུས་ཆུང་བ་ལ་བརྙས་བཅོས་བྱེད། སེམས་ཅན་ལ་བློ་སྦྱོང་འབྱུང་བ་ལ་མི་སྦྱོང་། གཉེན་གྲོགས་ལ་བཟོད་དགྲ་ལ་བཟོད་པ་མི་སྒོམ་པ་ལྟ་བུ་ཕྱོགས་རེ་སྤངས་ནས་ཕྱོགས་སུ་མ་ལྷུང་བར་བྱེད་དགོས་གསུངས་སོ། ༈ དམ་ཚིག་གཉིས་པ་ནི། །འདུན་པ་བསྒྱུར་ལ་རང་སོར་བཞག ཅེས་པས་དེ་སྔ་ཕན་ཆད་ནང་སེམས་ཀྱི་ཐོག་ནས། རང་གཅེས་པར་འཛིན་གཞན་མི་གཅེས་པའི་འདུན་པ་དེ་བསྒྱུར་ལ་སེམས་ཅན་གཞན་གཅེས་པར་བཟུང་ཞིང་། དེ་ཡང་ཕྱིའི་སྤྱོད

༄༅། །རྒྱལ་ལ་མི་ངོམས་པར་ཆོས་བྱེད་བཟང་ངན་གཞན་ཐམས་ཅད་ལ་མཐུན་པར་རང་གི་སྤྱོད་པ་སོ་ཐུབ་པར་བཞག་སྟེ། ནང་བསམ་པས་བདག་གཞན་བརྗེ་བ་སོགས་བྱང་སེམས་སློམ་པའི་རྣལ་འབྱོར་ལ་སྐད་ཅིག་ཙམ་ཡང་འབྲལ་བ་མེད་པས་ཉམས་ལེན་གོམས་ཤུགས་ལ་ཧ་མགྱོགས་ཤོས་བཞིན་ས་ཚོད་ཆེ་བར་བྱ་དགོས་གསུངས། གསུམ་པ། །ཡན་ལག་ཉམས་པ་བརྗོད་མི་བྱ། ཞེས་པས་རང་ཉིད་མི་གཤིས་ངན་པའམ་ཕྲག་དོག་གི་དབང་གིས། གཞན་པ་ཕོ་མོ་རྒན་གཞོན་སུ་འདྲ་ཡིན་ཀྱང་ལུས་ཀྱི་ཡན་ལག་ཉམས་པ་ཞར་བ། སྡུ་རྟ། ལྐུག་པ་སོགས་ཀྱི་སྐྱོན་ནས་འབོད་པ་དང་། ཆོས་ཀྱི་ཡན་ལག་ཉམས་པ་བསླབ་འཆལ་གྲྭ་ལོག་ དགོར་ཟན། ཐོབ་རྫུན་སོགས་མི་སྙན་པའི་ཚིག་སྒྲོག་ལ་བབས་ཀྱང་དུས་ནམ་ཡང་བརྗོད་པར་མི་བྱ། རང་ལའང་སྐད་མི་རུང་སྟེ་དལ་འབྱོར་ནི་ཐར་པའི་རྟེན་ཡིན་པ་དང་། གདན་གསུམ་ཚང་བའི་ལྷའི་དཀྱིལ་འཁོར་ཡིན་པར་གསུངས་པའི་ཕྱིར་རོ། བཞི་པ། །གཞན་ཕྱོགས་གང་ཡང་མི་བསམ་མོ། ཞེས་པས་ཕྱི་ནས་ཚིག་དང་རྣམ་འགྱུར་ངན་པ་འདོར་བ་མ་ཟད། ནང་སེམས་ཀྱིས་ཀྱང་གཞན་ཕྱོགས་ཀྱི་སྐྱོན་གང་ཡང་མི་བསམ་མོ། གལ་ཏེ་གཞན་གྱི་སྐྱོན་མཐོང་ཐོས་བྱུང་ན་འང་། རང་ཉིད་འདི་ལས་ངན་པའི་སྐྱོན་གྱི་ཕུང་པོ་ཡིན་པར་བསམ་ནས། བདག་བས་གཞན་གཅེས་སོགས་བློ་སྦྱོང་གི་ཕན་ཡོན་བསམ་ནས་རང་གཤིས་ངན་པ་ཅི་ཡོད་ལྡོག་ཐབས་ལ་འབད། ལྷག་པར་རང་གི་རྩ་བའི་བླ་མ་རྣམས་ཀྱི་སྐྱོན་ལ་མི་རྟོག སྣང་བ་དག་ན་རྒྱན་མོའི་ཁྲི་སོ་ལས་རིང་བསྲིལ་བྱུང་བའི་དཔེ་དང་། དད་པ་དང་བཀའ་དྲིན་བརྗོད། སྣང་བ་མ་དག་པར་གྱུར་ནས་སྐྱོན་མཐོང་ཡང་ངེས་པ་མེད་དེ། ལྷ་སྦྱིན་དང་། དགེ་སློང་ལེགས་པའི་སྐར་མ། མུ་སྟེགས་པ་ཁ་ཅིག་གིས་སངས་རྒྱས་ལ་སྐྱོན་མཐོང་བ་དང་འདྲ་བསམ་སྟེ་རང་སེམས་མ་དད་པ་དང་ལོག་ལྟ་ཆར་བཅད་ནས། དུས་སྙིགས་མར་མདོ་རྒྱུད་ནས་གསུངས་པའི་མཚན་ལྡན་གྱི་བཤེས་གཉེན་དཀོན་སྟབས་རང་གི་བླ་མ་དེ་ལའང་སྐྱོན་ཡོད་རུང་མེད་རུང་དག་སྣང་བྱེད་ནུས་ན་རང་གི་དམ་ཚིག་གི་ནོར་བུ་ལ་བྱི་དོར་བྱུང་བ་ཡིན་ནོ། ལྔ་པ། །ཉོན་མོངས་གང་ཆེ་སྔོན་ལ་སྦྱང་། ཞེས་པས་རང་དོན་ཆགས་སྡང་ལྷུར་ལེན་པ་བདག་ལྟ་བུ་མ་ཡིན་པས་ནི། རང་གི་ཉམས་ལེན་ལམ་དུ་འགྲོ་མི་བཅུག་ཅིང་རང་སེམས་རྒྱབ་ཟེང་ངེ་བ་ཆོར་མ་ལྷ་བུར་སྡོད་དགོས་པ་འམ། སྤྱིལ་ལྷ་བུ་བྲིལ་ཚུབས་སེ་སྡོད་དགོས་པ། གྲོགས་ཁྲིམ་མཆེས་སོགས་མི་དད་པའི་ཕྲག་དོག་སོགས་རང་

ཉེར་གསུམ་

༄༅། །རྒྱུད་ལ་ཉོན་མོངས་གང་ཆེ་བ་ཡོད་པ་དེའི་ཐོག་ཏུ་གཉེན་པོ་ཐམས་ཅད་སྤྱུངས་ཏེ། ཉོན་མོངས་ཤུགས་ཆེ་བ་དེ་སྔོན་ལ་སྦྱངས། དེ་བཞིན་ཉོན་མོངས་འཕེལ་ཞིང་དགེ་བ་ལ་མིག་ལྟོས་ངན་པ་བྱེད་པའི་གྲོགས་ངན་པའང་དང་པོ་ནས་སྤྱངས་བ་ལ་བསླབ། དྲུག་པ། །འབྲས་བུར་རེ་བ་ཐམས་ཅད་སྤྱངས། ཞེས་པས་ཡར་ཞིང་དམ་པ་ལ་མཆོད་འབུལ། མ་རྣམ་ཐག་ལ་ཕན་གྲོགས་སོགས། མདོར་ན་དགེ་བའི་རྩ་བ་རྒྱ་ཆེ་ཆུང་གང་བགྱིད་ཀྱང་འབྲས་བུ་སྙན་གྲགས་སོགས་རང་དོན་ཡིད་བྱེད་ཀྱི་རེ་བ་ཐམས་ཅད་སྤྱངས། བདུན་པ། །དུག་ཅན་གྱི་ཟས་སྤྱངས། ཞེས་པས་དུག་བསྲེས་པ་ཅན་གྱི་ཟས་ཟོས་ན་འཆི་བ་ལྟར་དངོས་པོ་བདེན་འཛིན་དང་། བདག་འཛིན་མ་རིག་པ་སོགས་ཉོན་མོངས་པས་ཀུན་ནས་བསླངས་པའི་དགེ་བ་ཐམས་ཅད་ཐར་པའི་རྒྱུར་མི་འགྲོ་ཞིང་འཁོར་བར་འཆིང་ནས་སྡུག་བསྔལ་བསྐྱེད་པས། དམ་པ་གསུམ་སོགས་གཉེན་པོས་བརྩིས་ཟིན་པར་བྱས་ནས་དགག་བྱ་དེ་དག་སྤྱངས་བ་ལ་བསླབ། གཞན་ཡང་ལུས་ལ་ནད་བསྐྱེད་པའི་བཟའ་བཏུང་དང་། ལོག་འཚོ་སོགས་སྤྱངས་བ་ལ་འཁང་གོ །བརྒྱད་པ། །གཞུང་བཟང་པོ་མ་བསྟེན། ཕྱི་ལ་མི་གཞུང་བཟང་པོ་ལྟར་བྱེད་ནས་ནང་གནག་པའི་

45

གཡོ་རྒྱུའི་གཤིས་ཀ་ངན་པ་དང་། སྔར་མི་དགའ་བའི་རྒྱུ་མཚན་ཞེ་ལ་བཞག་ནས་འཁོན་དུ་བཟུང་བ་སོགས་བློ་སྦྱོང་ཉམས་པའི་ངང་ཚུལ་སྤྱངས། ཐེག་པའི་གྲོགས་པོ་ལ་གཞུང་བཟང་པོས་ཡང་ཡང་ལྷན་འཛོག་བྱས་ན་དེའི་སྐྱོན་རང་ལ་འགོ་ནས་སྔར་ཡོད་པའི་སྤྱོད་པ་བཟང་པོ་ཇེ་འགྲིབ་ཏུ་འགྲོ་བས་སྙིང་ནས་མ་བསྟེན་གསུངས། དགུ་པ། །ཤགས་ངན་མི་རྒོད། ཅེས་པས་བློ་སྦྱོང་སྒོམ་པ་པོས། རྩེ་མོ་ཀུ་རེའི་ཚུལ་གྱིས་གཞན་ལ་མཚང་འདྲུ་བ་སོགས་ཁ་ཤགས་ངན་པ་འགྲེད་པར་མི་བྱ་སྟེ་དམུ་རྒོད་ཀྱི་ངང་ཚུལ་སྤྱངས། བཅུ་པ། །འཕྲང་མ་སྒུགས། ཞེས་པས་དགྲས་ལམ་འཕྲང་ནས་སྒུགས་ནས་གསོད་པ་ལྟར། སྔར་རང་དང་རང་གི་ཕྱོགས་ལ་གནོད་པ་བྱས་པ་ལོ་མང་ལོན་ཀྱང་མ་བརྗེད་པར་ཞེ་ནས་སྒུགས་ཏེ། སྐབས་འགྲིགས་པ་དང་ལུས་ངག་གང་རུང་གི་ཆ་ནས་ཚིག་ངན་དང་། རྡོ་དབྱུག་སོགས་གནོད་ལེན་སྒྲིལ་བར་མི་བྱ། སྒྲི་བཤོལ་མེད་ནས་དགྲ་བོ་དངོས་ནི་ནང་གི་བདག་འཛིན་ཡིན་པར་གསུངས་པས་བཟོད་པ་དང་སྟོང་ཉིད་ཟབ་མོའི་རལ་གྲི་རང་གི་ཞེ་སྡང་དང་འཁོན་འཛིན་གྱི་རྐེ་ལ་བཏེག །བཅུ་གཅིག་པ། །གནད་ལ་མི་དབབ། ཅེས་པས་རང་གི་འགྲན་ཟླ་ལྟ་བུའི་མི་གཞན་ཆམ་ལ་འབེབས་ཆེད་ཁ་ཡོག་རྒྱག་པ་

46

༄༅། །དང་། མི་སྨྲུན་དུ་ངོ་ཚ་དམའ་འབེབས། མི་དང་མི་མ་ཡིན་གྱི་ཚེ་སྲོག་འཕྲོག་པར་འདོད་པའི་ངན་སྔགས་དང་མཐུ་བྱེད་པ་སོགས་དེའི་ཁ་རྗེ་ལུས་སྲོག་ལ་གནོད་
པའི་ལས་ངན་པའི་རིགས་མི་བརྩམ་པ་སྟེ་ཁོའི་ལུས་དང་སེམས་ལ་གནོད་པའི་གནད་ཐོག་ལ་མི་དབབ། བཅུ་གཉིས་པ། །མཛོ་ཁལ་གླང་ལ་མི་འབྱོ། ཞེས་པས་མཛོ་ལ་འགེལ་རྒྱུའི་ཁལ་
ལྗི་བོ་གླང་ལ་བཀལ་བ་ལྟ་བུའི་རང་གི་ལས་ཀ་དཀའ་ཚེགས་ཅན་ལྗི་བོ་གཞན་མགོ་ལ་མི་འབྱོ་སྟེ་མི་འགེལ་བའམ། རྐུ་རྫུན་སོགས་ཉེས་པའི་རིགས་དང་། ཐན་བཅའ་ལག་ཆག་བཀྱུམ་བྱུས་
པ་སོགས་ཀྱི་ལེ་ལོག་གཞན་གྱི་སྟེང་དུ་འགེལ་བར་མི་བྱ། བཅུ་གསུམ་པ། །མགྲོགས་ཀྱི་རྩེ་མི་གཏོད། ཅེས་པས་དྲ་རྒྱུགས་པའི་ཚེ་སུ་མགྲོགས་ཀྱི་བང་རྩལ་འགྲན་པ་ལྟ་བུའི་མི་མང་པོའི་
ནང་ནས་རང་ལ་ཟམ་ནོར་མང་བ་དང་། ཆེ་བཀྲུག་བཀུར་སྟི་ལེགས་ཤོམ་ཐོབ་ཐབས་དང་མ་བྱུང་ན་ཁོང་ཁྲོ་བྱེད་པ། སྒྱི་རྩམ་དགོར་སོགས་ལ་གཞན་གྱིས་མོས་མཐུན་མེད་པར་རང་གིས་སུ་
མགྲོགས་ལྟ་བུའི་ལེགས་ཤོམ་ལེན་པ་སོགས་བྱེད་པ་ལ་གླེ་རྩེ་མི་གཏོད། བཅུ་བཞི་པ། །ལྷ་ལོག་མི་བྱ། ཞེས་པས་རང་གིས་བླ་སྦྱོང་སོགས་དམ་པའི་ཆོས་ཉམས་སུ་ལེན་པ་ཐམས་ཅད།

ཆེ་འདིའི་དོན་འཇིག་རྟེན་ཆོས་བརྒྱད་སྒྲུབ་ཐབས་ཁོ་ནའི་ཆེད་དུ་ཤོར་ན། ཟས་ཟ་ཉེས་ནས་ལྷ་བ་ལོག་སྟེ་གཤའ་སྒྱུགས་བྱེད་པ་ལྟ་བུ་ཡིན་པས་དེ་ལྟར་མི་བྱ། བཅོ་ལྔ་པ། །ལྷ་བདུད་དུ་མི་
དབབ། ཅེས་པས་བླ་སྦྱོང་སྒོམ་བཞིན་རང་རྒྱུད་ཐེ་གྲོང་། གཞན་ལ་མཐོང་ཆུང་དང་དམའ་འབེབས། རང་ལ་མཆོག་འཛིན་སོགས་ཀྱི་རྒྱུར་འཆོར་བ། གཞན་ཡང་ཆོས་སྐྱོང་སོགས་དྲག་པོ་
སྒྲུབ་པ་རང་དང་རང་གི་གཉེན་གྲོགས་ལ་གནོད་པ་རྒྱུ་མཚན་དུ་བྱེད་ནས་དགྲ་བོ་དེ་བཏྒགས་པའི་ཆེད་དུ་བྲད་པ་སོགས་ནི་ལྷ་ཡེ་ཤེས་པ་ཡིན་ཀྱང་ཀུན་སློང་ཞེ་སྡང་དུ་ཤོར་བས་དེ་ལྟར་བདུད་དུ་མི་
དབབ་སྟེ་མི་བསྒྱུར། བཅུ་དྲུག་པ། །སྐྱིད་ཀྱི་ཡན་ལག་ཏུ་སྡུག་མ་ཚོལ། །ཞེས་པ་ཏེ། རང་གི་འགྲན་ཡ་མེད་པར་གྱུར་ན་རང་ལ་དེའི་བསོད་བདེ་དང་བཀུར་སྟི་ཡོང་སྙམ་པ་དང་། རང་
དང་རང་གི་ཕྱོགས་མ་གཏོགས་གཞན་ལ་མི་བདེ་བ་བྱུང་ན་ལེགས་སྙམ་པ་དང་། ཆོས་པ་སོགས་བཟང་རྩུགས་རྫིག་པོ་བཟུང་ན་ཟས་ནོར་དང་སྙན་གྲགས་འོང་སྙམ་པ་སོགས་བསམ་སྦྱོར་བློ་
སྦྱོང་གི་ཆོས་དང་མི་མཐུན་པ་ཐམས་ཅད་ནི་རང་སྐྱིད་ཀྱི་ཆེད་དུ་གཞོམ་ནའང་འབྲས་བུ་ཡན་ལག་ཏུ་སྡུག་བཙལ་བ་ལྟ་བུ་ཡིན་པས་དེ་ལྟར་དུས་ནམ་ཡང་མ་ཚོལ་ཏེ་བྱ་མི་རུང་གསུངས་སོ། དེ་

༄༅། །ལྷར་བློ་སྦྱོང་གི་དམ་ཚིག་བཅུ་དྲུག་ནི། ཐེག་པ་གཞན་གྱི་ལམ་གྱི་སྤྱོག་སྟོམ་པ་ཡིན་པ་ལྷར་བློ་སྦྱོང་ཉམས་སུ་ལེན་མཁན་གྱིས་དམ་ཚིག་འདི་དག་ལས་སྲུང་
གཅིག་མ་འགལ་བར་དྲན་ཤེས་བག་ཡོད་ཀྱིས་སྲུངས་ཤིང་གལ་ཏེ་འགལ་བར་གྱུར་ན་གང་འགལ་བ་དེ་ཉིད་ཡིད་ཡུལ་དུ་བླངས་ཏེ། བདག་གིས་འདིས་གཙོས། སེམས་ཅན་ཐམས་ཅད་ཀྱི་
བསམ་སྦྱོར་ཕྱིན་ཅི་ལོག་ཏུ་གྱུར་པའི་སྡིག་པ་མི་དགེ་བ་ཅི་མཆིས་པ་མཉམ་དུ་བཤགས་པ་ལ་འབད་དོ། དེ་ལྟར་ཐེག་ཆེན་ཆོས་ཀྱི་སྙིང་པོ་བདག་གཞན་མཉམ་བརྗེའི་བློ་སྦྱོང་ཟབ་མོ་ཆེ་གཅིག་ཏུ་
ཉམས་སུ་ལེན་པ་ལ་ཕན་པའི་བླང་དོར་གྱི་བསླབ་བྱ་ཉི་ཤུ་རྩ་གཉིས་གསུངས་ཏེ། དང་པོ། །རྣལ་འབྱོར་ཐམས་ཅད་གཅིག་གིས་བྱ། ཞེས་པས་ཆོས་གཞན་གྱི་ལུགས་ཟ་ཉལ་སོགས་ལ་རྣལ་
འབྱོར་སོ་སོར་ཡོད་པ་རྣམས་འདིར་མི་དགོས་ཤིང་བློ་སྦྱོང་ཉམས་སུ་ལེན་མཁན་གྱིས་གང་དང་ཅི་བྱེད་པ་ཐམས་ཅད་གཞན་ལ་ཕན་ཐབས་ཀྱི་བསམ་བློ་དུང་ངེ་བ་བློ་སྦྱོང་ཁོན་དུས་ནམ་ཡང་མ་
བརྗེད་པར་བྱེད་པའི་རྣལ་འབྱོར་གཅིག་གིས་དུས་ཀུན་ལ་ཚོག་པར་བྱ་ཞིང་ནུས་ན་འདི་པའི་ལུགས་ཟ་ཉལ་སོགས་སྤྱོད་ལམ་གྱི་རྣལ་འབྱོར་གང་བྱ་མོས་པ་བློ་སྦྱོང་ཐུན་བརྒྱད་སོགས་ལས་རྟོགས་

པར་བྱའོ། གཉིས་པ། །ལོག་གནོན་ཐམས་ཅད་གཅིག་གིས་བྱ། ཞེས་པས་ཆོས་བསྒྲུབས་བཞིན་གནས་སྐབས་རང་ལ་ནད་ཚ་རྐྱེན་ཆག་མང་བ། མི་ཁ་ལེ་ཡོག་ལྷུང་བ། མཐུན་རྐྱེན་
གྲོགས་སོགས་ཇེ་ཉུང་། ནང་གི་ཉོན་མོངས་ཆེ་རུ་འགྲོ་བ། ཆོས་ཀྱིས་སུན་པ་སོགས་ཅི་ཡང་ཡོང་སྲིད་ཅིང་དེ་ལ་བརྟེན་ནས་ཐེ་ཚོམ་དང་སྙིང་ལྕུག་པ། ལུས་ངག་ཡིད་ཀྱིས་དགེ་བ་བསྒྲུབ་མི་
འདོད་པ་སོགས་འགལ་རྐྱེན་བར་ཆད་ཆེན་པོ་བྱུང་ན། འཇིག་རྟེན་ན་བདག་ལྟ་བུ་ཆོས་ལ་ཕྱིན་ཅི་ལོག་ཏུ་གྱུར་པ་མང་པོ་ཡོད་པས་དེ་དག་གིས་གཙོས་པའི་སེམས་ཅན་ཐམས་ཅད་ཀྱི་རྣམ་རྟོག
ངན་པ་ཐམས་ཅད་བདག་གི་འདིའི་ཐོག་ཏུ་བླངས་ཏེ་བདག་གི་ལུས་ལོངས་སྤྱོད་དགེ་བ་ཀུན་དེ་དག་ལ་འབུལ་བས་དེ་རྣམས་བསམ་སྦྱོར་ཕྱིན་ཅི་མ་ལོག་པའི་ལམ་དུ་ཞུགས་པར་བསམ་པ་ནི།
ལོག་གནོན་ནམ་འགལ་རྐྱེན་དེ་དག་བཟློག་ཐབས་ཀྱི་གཉེན་པོ་ཐམས་ཅད་ཀྱི་མཆོག་ཏུ་གྱུར་པ་ཡིན་ཅིང་རང་ཡང་ཆོས་ལ་སྙིང་ལྕུག་དང་ཐེ་ཚོམ་སོགས་སྐྱང་བའི་དམ་བཅའ་ལེན་པ་སོགས་
གཞན་ཕན་གཏོང་ལེན་གྱི་བློ་གཅིག་གིས་ཚོག་པར་བྱ། གཞན་ཡང་བྱང་ཆུབ་སེམས་སྒོམ་པའི་ཕན་ཡོན་ཤིན་ཏུ་རྒྱ་ཆེན་པོ་མདོ་སྡེ་སོགས་ལས་འབྱུང་བ་མཐའ་བར་བྱ། གསུམ་པ། །ཐོག

ཉེརྡུག

༄༅། །མཐའ་གཉིས་ལ་བྱ་བ་གཉིས། ཞེས་པ་སྟེ། ཐོག་མར་ཞོག་ཀ་མལ་ནས་ལྡང་བ་ན། ཆོས་ལྡན་གྱི་མི་སྐྱ་ཕོ་མོ་ཡིན་ན། དེ་རིང་དམ་པའི་ཆོས་དང་མི་མཐུན་པའི་གཞན་ལ་འཁྲུག་ཡོང་། དུད་འགྲོ་ཉམས་ཆུང་རིགས་ལ་བརྡུང་གསོད། ཆང་རག་དུ་བ། མནའ་དམོད་མོ། མགོ་བསྐོར་ཁ་བསླུ་སོགས་མི་དགེ་བའི་ལས་མི་བྱེད་སྙམ་དུ་དམ་བཅའ། སེར་མོའི་རིགས་ཡིན་ན་དེ་རིང་བསླབ་པ་ལ་བག་ཡོད་དྲན་ཤེས་ཐོག་བདག་གཅེས་པར་འཛིན་ནས་གཞན་ལ་བསམ་སྦྱོར་ངན་པ་མི་བྱེད་ཅིང་གཞན་གཅེས་པར་འཛིན་པ་མ་ཉམས་པར་བྱ་སྙམ་པ་དང་༎ སྤྱི་ཆར་ནུས་ན་དུས་དྲན་བརྟེན་པ་སོགས་ཀྱིས་ཐབས་བཙལ། གང་ལྟར་བྱང་ཆུབ་སེམས་སྨོན་ཀློང་ནས་བཟུང་ཉིན་མོ་དང་། ཐུན་ཆོད་སོགས་བྱ་བ་གང་གི་ཐོག་མར་གཞན་ཕན་སེམས་བསྐྱེད་ཀྱིས་རྩིས་ཟིན་པར་བྱེད་ནས་དྲན་པ་རྒྱུན་ཆགས་བརྟེན། ཐུན་གྱི་མཐའ་མའམ། དོ་ནུབ་ཉལ་ཁ་དེ་རིང་དགེ་སྡིག་གང་བྱས་འདུག་རང་རྒྱུད་ལ་བརྟགས་ནས་ཐེག་པ་ཆེན་པོའི་ཆོས་དང་འགལ་བ་བྱུང་འདུག་ན་བཤགས་པ་དང་དགེ་བ་བྱུང་ན་གཞན་དོན་དུ་བསྔོ་བ་སྟེ། དེ་ལྟར་ཐོག་མཐའ་གཉིས་པོ་ལ་དགེ་མི་དགེ་རྩི་བགྲང་གི་བྱ་བ་གཉིས་ལ་འབད་དགོས་པའོ། བཞི་

51

པ༎ །གཉིས་པོ་གང་བྱུང་བཟོད་པར་བྱ། ཞེས་པས་བདག་ལྟ་བུའི་ཅོལ་ཆུང་སྐྱིད་རྒྱགས་ཆེན་པོ་བྱུང་ན་སྐྱིད་མི་ཐེག་ནས་དམ་སྡོམ་སོགས་ཆོས་སྤྱོད་བག་མེད་དུ་འདོར་བ་དང་། ཡང་ན་ལུས་སེམས་ལ་སྡུག་བསྔལ་མང་པོས་རྒྱུན་མ་ཆད་པར་མནར་བ་བྱུང་ན། སྡུག་མི་ཐེག་ནས་ཆོས་འདོར་བ་སོགས་སྐྱིད་སྡུག་མི་ཐེག་པའི་བར་ཆད་གཉིས་པོ་གང་བྱུང་ཡང་། དེས་དབང་དུ་མི་བཏང་ཞིང་སྐྱིད་པ། ཚེ་སྔོན་བསོད་ནམས་ཕྲན་བུ་བསགས་པའི་འབྲས་བུའམ། བླ་མ་དཀོན་མཆོག་གི་བྱིན་རླབས་ཡིན་སྲིད། སྡུག་པོ་རང་གི་ལས་ངན་འཁོར་བའམ། ནག་ཕྱོགས་ཀྱི་བར་ཆད་ཡིན་སྲིད་པས། གང་ལྟ་བུ་བྱུང་ཡང་བྱམས་དང་སྙིང་རྗེས་ལེ་ལན་འཇལ་དགོས་སྙམ་ཞིང་སྐྱིད་སྡུག་ཅི་བྱུང་རོ་སྙོམས། མདོར་ན། མི་ཡ་རབས་སྤྱོད་བཟང་བྱང་ཆུབ་སེམས་དཔའ་བྱེད་པ་ལ་བཟོད་པའི་གོ་ཆ་བརྟན་པར་བྱ་དགོས་གསུངས། བཞི་པ། །གཉིས་པོ་སྲོག་དང་བསྡོམས་ནས་བསྲུང་། ཞེས་པས་དམ་པའི་ཆོས་སྤྱིའི་དམ་ཚིག་གཞན་གནོད་གཞི་བཅས་སྤངས་ཤིང་གཞན་ཕན་གཞི་བཅས་བསྒྲུབ་རྒྱུ་དང་། ཁྱད་པར་འདིར་བསྟན་བློ་སྦྱོང་གི་དམ་ཚིག་རྣམས་ཏེ། དེ་ལྟར་དམ་ཚིག་གཉིས་པོ་ཉམས་ན་འདི་ཕྱིའི་བདེ་བ་མི་འབྱུང་བ་དང་། ཁྱད་པར་བདག་གཞན་བརྗེ་

52

༄༅། །བའི་བྱང་ཆུབ་ཀྱི་སེམས་སྒོམ་པའི་ལམ་གྱི་གཞིར་ཡང་མེད་དུ་མི་རུང་བས་སྔོག་དང་བསྔོས་ནས་བསྲུང་དགོས་ཏེ། འགའ་ཞིག་གིས་དཀོན་མཆོག་གསུམ་དང་
གཞན་ཕན་བྱང་ཆུབ་ཀྱི་སེམས་མ་སྐྱངས་ན་གསོད་ཟེར་ནས་མཚོན་རྩེ་སྙིང་གར་གཏད་ཀྱང་མི་སྤོང་བ་ལྟ་བུའོ། དྲུག་པ། །དཀའ་བ་གསུམ་ལ་བསླབ་པར་བྱ། ཞེས་གསུངས་ཏེ། བདག་ལྟ་
བུ་ཉོན་མོངས་ལ་གོམས་པའི་དབང་གིས། དུག་ལྔ་སོགས་གང་རུང་དང་པོ་སྐྱེས་མ་ཐག་ཏུ་ད་ལྟ་སྐྱེས་བྱུང་སྙམ་པ་ལྟ་བུས་སྐད་ཅིག་མར་ངོ་ཤེས་པ་དཀའ། བར་དུ་རྒྱུན་འཆོགས་ཏེ་ཞེ་སྡང་
སོགས་སྐྱེས་པ་གཉེན་པོ་བྱམས་པ་སོགས་ཀྱིས་དེ་མ་ཐག་མགོ་གནོན་པར་དཀའ། མཐར་དེ་ལྟར་མི་སྐྱེ་བ་ཉོན་མོངས་པའི་རྒྱུན་གཅོད་པར་དཀའ་བས། ཞེ་སྡང་སོགས་ཉོན་མོངས་པ་དང་པོ་མ
སྐྱེས་པའི་སྔོན་ནས་དྲན་པའི་བྱ་རས་ཡེངས་མེད་དུ་བཟུང་། དེ་ལྟར་སྒྲིམ་པའི་དབང་གིས་སྐྱེས་མ་ཐག་རིག་སྟེ། དེ་གསུམ་གྱི་དབང་དུ་མཛོར་བ་ལ་བསླབ་པར་བྱ། བདུན་པ། །རྒྱུ་ཡི་གཙོ་
བོ་རྣམ་གསུམ་བླང་། ཞེས་པས་བློ་སྦྱོང་སོགས་དམ་པའི་ཆོས་ཚུལ་བཞིན་ཉམས་སུ་ལོན་པའི་རྒྱུ་ཡི་གཙོ་བོ་རྣམ་པ་གསུམ་སྟེ། ལམ་སྟོན་བླ་མ་ཚད་ལྡན་དང་། ཆོས་ཉམས་སུ་ལེན་པར

འདོད་པའི་སྤྲོ་བ་དང་། མཐུན་རྐྱེན་ཟས་གོས་སོགས་རྙེད་སླ་བ་བཅས་གལ་ཆེ་བས་རང་ལ་འཛོམས་ན་དགའ་བ་བསྒོམ་ཞིང་གཞན་འཛོམས་པ་ལ་ཡི་རངས་བྱེད། སླན་ཆད་ཀྱང་གང་དུ་བཙལ
སླ་བ་དང་དུ་བླང་། རང་ལ་དཔལ་འབྱོར་ཡོད་ན་ཆོས་པ་གཞན་ལའང་དེ་ལྟར་མཐུན་རྐྱེན་བསྒྲུབ། བརྒྱད་པ། །ཉམས་པ་མེད་པ་རྣམ་གསུམ་བསྒོམ། ཞེས་པས་རང་ལ་བློ་སྦྱོང་སོགས་བྱང་
ཆུབ་སེམས་སྟོན་པའི་བླ་མ་ལ་མོས་གུས་ཉམས་པ་མེད་པ་དང་། བདག་གཞན་བརྗེ་བའི་བྱང་ཆུབ་སེམས་བསྒོམ་པ་ལ་ལོ་ཟླ་བ་ག་ཚད་སོང་ཡང་སྐྱུན་པ་དང་དགའ་སེམས་རྒྱུད་དུ་དོར་ནས་དད་
པ་དང་སྤྲོ་བ་ཉམས་པ་མེད་པ་དང་། བློ་སྦྱོང་གི་དམ་ཚིག་དང་བསླབ་བྱ་ནམ་ཡང་མི་བརྗེད་པས་སྤྱངས་བླངས་ཉམས་པ་མེད་པ་རྣམ་པ་གསུམ་ལ་བག་ཡོད་དྲན་ཤེས་ཀྱིས་མི་འབྲལ་བར་བསྒོམ
ཞིང་ལག་ཏུ་བླང་། བླ་མ་ལ་དད་གུས་ཉམས་ན་ཡོན་ཏན་སྐྱེ་བའི་སྒོ་འགག བློ་སྦྱོང་ཉམས་སུ་ལེན་པ་ལ་དད་གུས་དང་དགའ་སྤྲོ་ཉམས་ན་བྱང་ཆུབ་སེམས་སྐྱེ་བའི་གནས་མེད། བསླབ་པ་ལ
བག་ཡོད་ཉམས་ན་ཡོན་ཏན་སྐྱེ་བའི་གཞི་མེད་པར་གསུངས། །དགུ་པ། །འབྲལ་མེད་གསུམ་དང་ལྡན་པར་བྱ། ཞེས་པས་སྡིག་གཅོད་པ་སོགས་ལུས་ཀྱི་མི་དགེ་བ་སྤངས་ཤིང་ཕྱག་དང་

༄༅། །བསྐོར་བ་དང་། ལྷ་ཁང་གི་ཕྱི་ནང་དང་མཆོད་པ་སོགས་གཙང་སྦྲ། བླ་མ་དང་ཕ་མའི་ཞབས་ཏོག ནད་པ་དབུལ་ཕོངས་སོགས་ལ་སྨན་དང་ཟས་གོས་གནས
མལ་སྦྱིན་པ་བཙས་ཕན་པ་གང་ཐུབ་ཀྱིས་ལུས་དགེ་བ་ལ་འབྲལ་བ་མེད་པ་དང་། རྫུན་དང་ཕྲ་མ་སོགས་ངག་གི་མི་དགེ་བ་སྤྱངས་ཤིང་ངག་གིས་ཁ་ཏོན་བཟླས་བརྗོད། ནུས་ན་ཉིན་རེ་རེ་བཞིན
ཀླུང་གི་གཏོར་ལེན་བརྒྱ་རྩ་སོགས་དང་། ཆོས་འཆད་རྩོམ་སོགས་རང་གིས་གང་ནུས་ཀྱིས་ངག་དགེ་བ་ལ་འབྲལ་བ་མེད་པ་དང་། གནོད་སེམས་སོགས་ཡིད་ཀྱི་མི་དགེ་བ་སྤྱངས་ནས་ཡིད
ངེས་འབྱུང་དང་། བྱང་ཆུབ་ཀྱི་སེམས། སྟོང་ཉིད་ཀྱི་ལྟ་བ་སོགས་ཡིད་དགེ་བ་དང་འབྲལ་བ་མེད་པ་གསུམ་དང་དུས་རྟག་ཏུ་ལྡན་པར་བྱའོ། བཅུ་པ། །ཡུལ་ལ་ཕྱོགས་མེད་དག་ཏུ་སྦྱང་།
ཞེས་པས་བྱམས་དང་སྙིང་རྗེས་གཏོང་ལེན་བསྒོམ་པའི་ཡུལ་ལ་དགྲ་དང་གཉེན། མི་དང་མི་མ་ཡིན་པ་སོགས་འདི་ལ་བསྒོམ། འདི་ལ་མི་བསྒོམ་སླམ་པའི་ཕྱོགས་རིས་མེད་པ་དག་ཏུ་སྦྱང
ངོ་༔ བཅུ་གཅིག་པ། །ཁྱབ་དང་གཏིང་འབྱོངས་ཀུན་ལ་གཅེས། ཞེས་པ་སྟེ། རང་གི་ལུས་ངག་ཡིད་ཀྱིས་བྱ་བ་ཅི་བགྱིད་པ་ཐམས་ཅད་ལ་བྱང་ཆུབ་སེམས་ཀྱི་ནས་ཁྱབ་པར་བྱ་ཞིང་དེའང

ཁ་ཙམ་དང་དྲན་ཙམ་མ་ཡིན་པར་སྙིང་ཁྲུང་རུས་པའི་གཏིང་ནས་ཉམས་སུ་ལེན་ཏེ་འབྱོངས་བའི་ཐབས་དུས་ཀུན་ལ་གཅེས་སོ། བཅུ་གཉིས་པ། །བགོལ་བ་རྣམས་ལ་རྟག་ཏུ་བསྒོམ། ཞེས་
གསུངས་ཏེ། རང་ལ་ཤིན་ཏུ་འཚེ་བའི་གཟུགས་ཅན་དང་གཟུགས་མེད་ཀྱི་དགྲ་དང་། དྲིན་ལན་ལོག་འཇལ་བྱེད་པ་སོགས་གནོད་བྱེད་ཚབ་ཆེ་བའི་རིགས་རང་གི་སེམས་ལ་གཟན་ཆེ་བ་གང་
ཡོད་པ་ཐམས་ཅད་ཟུར་དུ་བགོལ་བར་བྱ་ནས་དེ་རྣམས་ལ་ལྷག་པར་བྱམས་སྙིང་རྗེ་རྟག་ཏུ་བསྒོམ། དེ་བཞིན་དུ་རང་གི་སེམས་ལ་ངརྒྱལ་འཕེལ་བ་དང་ཆགས་པའི་ཡུལ། སེམས་ཡོད་དང
སེམས་མེད་ཀྱི་དངོས་པོ། བློ་རྣལ་དུ་མི་གནས་ཅིང་རྒོད་པར་བྱེད་པའི་རིགས་གང་ཡོད་པའང་ཟུར་དུ་བགོལ་ནས་འདུས་བྱས་མི་རྟག་པའི་རང་བཞིན་སྙིང་པོ་མེད་པའི་ཚུལ་དང་འཁོར་གསུམ
བདེན་མེད་རྒྱུ་མའི་དངོས་པོ་ལྟ་བུར་བསྒོམ་པས་སྦྱངས། བཅུ་གསུམ་པ། །རྐྱེན་གཞན་དག་ལ་ལྟོས་མི་བྱ། ཞེས་པས་མཚམས་བསྙེན་སྒྲུབ་སོགས་དགེ་སྦྱོར་གཞན་བྱེད་པ་ལ་ནད་མེད་པ
དང་འཚོ་བ་མཐུན་རྐྱེན་སོགས་དུ་མ་འཛོམས་དགོས་ཀྱང་། བློ་སྦྱོང་བསྒོམ་པ་ལ་དེ་འདྲའི་རྐྱེན་གཞན་དག་ལ་ལྟོས་པར་མི་བྱ་སྟེ་གང་མཐུན་རྐྱེན་མ་ཚང་བ་དང་འགལ་རྐྱེན་མང་བ་ཅི་བྱུང་བ་དེ

ཉེར་དགུ

༄༅། །ཉིད་མཐུན་པའི་རྐྱེན་དགེ་སྦྱོར་གྱི་གྲོགས། བདག་གཞན་བརྗེ་བའི་བྱང་ཆུབ་སེམས་ཀྱི་རྗེན་དུ་བསྒྱུར་དགོས་པ་ཡིན་ནོ། བཅུ་བཞི་པ། །ད་རེས་གཙོ་བོ་ཉམས་
སུ་བླངས། ཞེས་པས་ད་རེས་རང་གི་བསྒྲུབ་བྱ་ཆོས་དང་འཇིག་རྟེན་གཉིས་ལས་དལ་འབྱོར་གྱི་མི་ལུས་ཐོབ་པའི་དོན་གོ་གནད་བདེའི་འདུན་མ་དམ་པའི་ཆོས་གཙོ་བོར་བསྒྲུབ་དགོས་ཤིང་དེ་
ལའང་ཉམས་ལེན་རྣམ་གྲངས་མང་ཡང་། སངས་རྒྱས་ཀྱི་རྒྱུ་དངོས་བྱང་ཆུབ་ཀྱི་སེམས་སྒོམ་པ་ལས་ལྷག་པ་གཞན་མེད་པར་གསུངས། དེའི་སྙིང་པོའང་བློ་སྦྱོང་སྒོམ་པ་འདི་ཡིན་པས་ཆེ་འདི་
ལ་བྱ་བ་ཐམས་ཅད་ཀྱི་གཙོ་བོ་འདི་ཉིད་ཁོ་ན་ཉམས་སུ་བླང་། གཞན་ཡང་ཞི་བ་ལྷས། །ཞེ་སྡང་ལྟ་བུའི་སྡིག་པ་མེད། །བཟོད་པ་ལྟ་བུའི་དཀའ་ཐུབ་མེད། ཅེས་གསུངས་པ་ལྟར་ཉོན་མོངས་
ཀུན་གྱི་ནང་ནས་ཆེ་འདི་ཕྱི་གཏན་བརླགས་བྱེད་མཁན་གྱི་ལས་ཚབ་ཆེ་ཤོས་ཞེ་སྡང་དང་ཕྲག་དོག་ཡིན་སྟབས་འདི་འདུལ་བའི་ཐབས་གཙོ་བོ་བཟོད་པ་བསྒོམ་པ་ལ་ནན་ཏན་བཟུང་བའང་གནད་
གཅིག་གོ བཅོ་ལྔ་པ། །གོ་ལོག་མི་བྱ། ཞེས་གསུངས་པ་ནི་གོ་ལོག་དྲུག་སྤངས་ནས། གོ་བ་མ་ལོག་པ་དྲུག་བསྟེན་དགོས་པ་སྟེ། དང་པོ། ཆོ་གཅིག་ལ་བློ་སྦྱོང་སོགས་དམ་པའི་ཆོས་

57

ཁོན་བསྒྲུབ་པར་དམ་བཅས་པའི་གང་ཟག་གིས། དམ་པའི་ཆོས་ཀྱི་ཕྱོགས་ལ་དཀའ་སྤྱད། སྤྱ་ལངས་ཉལ་ཕྱི་ཙམ་མི་བཟོད་པར་སྡིག་པའི་ལས་ཀ་ཅི་ཡང་བྱེད་ནུས་པ་ནི་བཟོད་པ་གོ་ལོག །
ཁ་རག་སྒོམ་ཆུང་སོགས་བཀའ་གདམས་ཀྱི་བླ་མ་གོང་མ་རྣམས་ལྟར་གཏན་དུ་ཕན་པ་དམ་པའི་ཆོས་རྣམ་དག་འགྲུབ་ཐབས་ཀྱི་འདུན་པ་མི་བྱེད་པར་ཆེ་འདིའི་བདེ་སྐྱིད་སྣང་གྲགས་སོགས་
འཇིགས་རྟེན་ཆོས་བརྒྱད་ལ་འདུན་པ་བྱེད་པ་འདུན་པ་གོ་ལོག ཀུན་རྫོབ་དང་དོན་དམ་བྱང་ཆུབ་སེམས་སྒོམ་པའི་ཉམས་མྱོང་བདེ་བ་ཁྱད་པར་ཅན་གྱི་རོ་མི་མྱོང་བར་འཇིག་རྟེན་འདིའི་འདོད་
ཡོན་ནོར་རྫས་ཆང་རག་དུ་བ་སོགས་ཀྱི་རོ་ལ་ཞེན་པ་རོ་མྱོང་གོ་ལོག མི་དགེ་བ་བཅུ་དང་། འཇིག་རྟེན་གྱི་དམག་འཁྲུག་སོགས་སྡིག་པ་བྱེད་པ་ལ་སྙིང་རྗེ་མི་སྒོམ་པར་ཚུལ་ཁྲིམས་སྲུང་བའི་
དཀའ་སྤྱད་དང་ལྟོ་གོས་གཏམ་གསུམ་ལ་གྲོང་བསྐྱུར་ཏེ་ཆོས་ཕྱིར་དཀའ་ཐུབ་བྱེད་པ་ལ་སྙིང་རྗེ་སྒོམ་པ་སྙིང་རྗེ་གོ་ལོག རང་གི་ཁ་འོག་ཏུ་འདུ་བའི་གཉེན་གྲོགས་རྣམས་དཀར་པོ་དགེ་བའི་ཆོས་
སྤྱོད་པ་ལ་མི་སྦྱོར་བར་དགྲ་འདུལ་གཉེན་སྐྱོང་། གཡོ་རྒྱུ་ཁྲམ་གསུམ་སོགས་འཇིག་རྟེན་གྱི་ལས་ནག་པོ་ལ་སྦྱོར་བ་དོན་གཉེར་གྱི་སེམས་གོ་ལོག སངས་རྒྱས་ནས་སེམས་ཅན་བར་བདེ་སྐྱིད་

58

སུམ་ཅུ་ཐམ་པ

༄༅། །ཚེ་ཕྲ་ཅི་འབྱུང་བ་ནི་རང་རང་གི་དགེ་བ་ཆེ་ཕྲ་བྱས་པའི་འབྲས་བུ་ཡིན་པས་དེ་དག་ལ་དགའ་བས་རྗེས་སུ་ཡི་རང་མི་བྱེད་པར། ཕྲག་དོག་དང་མི་བདེ་བ་བྱུང་བ་ལ་དགའ་སྤྲོ་བྱེད་པ་རྗེས་སུ་ཡི་རང་གོ་ལོག་སྡེ་དུག་པོ་འདེབས་མཚོན་སྔོ་གསུམ་དགེ་བའི་ལས་དང་མི་མཐུན་པའི་གོ་ལོག་ངན་པ་ཐམས་ཅད་མི་བྱ་ཞིང་སྤང་བར་བྱའོ། བཅུ་དྲུག་པ། །རེས་འཇོག་མི་བྱ། ཞེས་པ་ནི། བདག་ལྟ་བུ། །སྲིད་རྒྱུགས་ཉི་མས་དྲོས་ན་ཆོས་པའི་གཟུགས། །རྐྱེན་ངན་ཐོག་ཏུ་བབས་ན་ཐ་མལ་པ། ཞེས་གསུངས་པ་བཞིན་མི་ཆོ་ཆོས་ལ་བརྟོན་པར་དམ་བཅས་ཀྱང་། མཐུན་རྐྱེན་འཛོམས། གཞན་གྱིས་བསྟེན་བཀུར་སོགས་ཕུན་སུམ་ཚོགས་པའི་སྐབས་སུ་ཆོས་བྱེད། དེ་དག་མ་བྱུང་བའི་དུས་སུ་མི་བྱེད་པ་ནི་གཉིང་ནས་ངེས་ཤེས་མ་སྐྱེས་པའི་རྟགས་ཡིན་འདུག་པས་དེ་ལྟར་རེས་འཇོག་མི་བྱ་བར་བཟང་ངན་ཅི་བྱུང་ཡང་བརྟོན་པ་ཆུ་བོའི་རྒྱུན་བཞིན་བསྐྱང་། བཅུ་བདུན་པ། །དོལ་ཆོད་དུ་སྤང་། ཞེས་པས་འགྲོ་འདུག་སྤྱོད་ལམ་ཐམས་ཅད་དུ་རྣམ་གཡེང་དང་ལོང་གཏམ་སོགས་ཀྱི་དབང་དུ་མི་བཏང་བར་བྱང་ཆུབ་སེམས་ལ་དོལ་ཆོད་དེ་འདུན་པ་རྩེ་གཅིག་ཏུ་དྲིལ་ནས་སྦྱང་བར་བྱ། བཅོ་བརྒྱད་པ། །རྟོག་དཔྱོད་གཉིས་ཀྱིས་ཐར་

བར་བྱ། ཞེས་གསུངས་ཏེ། དུས་རྒྱུན་དུ་རང་གི་ལུས་ངག་ཡིད་གསུམ་ལ་རྟོག་ཅིང་། ལེགས་ཉེས་ཅི་བྱ་བ་དཔྱོད་པར་བྱེད་པ་གཉིས་ཀྱི་བྱ་རས་བཟུང་པས། དེ་སྔོན་དང་མི་འདྲ་བའི་རང་སེམས་དུལ་བ་ལྟ་བུར་འདུག་ན། ད་དུང་ཉོན་མོངས་སྐྱེ་བའི་ཡུལ་ལ་དེ་སྔ་བཞིན་ཆགས་སྡང་དྲག་ཏུ་སྐྱེ་མི་སྐྱེ་བརྟག་ནས་སྐྱེ་བར་འདུག་ན་དེ་མ་ཐག་སྐྱོན་དེའི་ཐོག་ཏུ་གཉེན་པོ་ཐམས་ཅད་སྤུངས་ནས་ཉེས་པ་དེ་ལས་ཐར་བར་བྱ་དགོས་གསུངས། བཅུ་དགུ་པ། །ཡུས་མ་བསྒོམ། ཞེས་གསུངས་ཏེ། སེར་མོ་བ་དང་། སྐྱེ་བོ་ཕོ་མོ་སུ་ཡིན་ཀྱང་འདུ་འཚོགས་པ། ཚོགས་གསོག་སྒྲིབ་སྦྱོང་། གཞན་ལ་ལུས་ངག་ཡིད་ཀྱིས་ཕན་བཏགས་པ་སོགས་དགེ་བའི་བྱ་བ་བཟང་པོ་གང་བགྱིད་ཀྱང་། ལེགས་པོ་བྱས་པའི་ཡུས་གཞན་ལ་བཀྱི་ཞིང་ཡིད་ལ་མ་བསྒོམ་ན་ལེགས་ཏེ། ཐེག་པ་ཆེན་པོའི་རིགས་སད། རྐྱེན་དགེ་བའི་བཤེས་གཉེན་གྱིས་ཟིན། ཐབས་དེའི་གདམས་ངག་ཐོབ་ནས་ཆོས་བསྒྲུབ་པ་ནི་རང་དོན་ཡིན་པར་གསུངས་པས་སོ། ཉི་ཤུ་པ། །ཀོ་ལོང་མི་སྒོམ། ཞེས་པས་གྲ་རོགས་དང་གཡོག་འཁོར་སོགས་སུ་ཞིག་ཡིན་རུང་རང་གི་འདོད་མོས་ལ་འགལ་འཛུལ་ཅུང་ཟད་ཙམ་ཤོར་ན་དེ་འཕྲལ་སྤྱོ་ཐུང་བས། མིག་ལོག་སོགས་མི་

ཤོ་གཅིག

༄༅། ། དགའ་བའི་རྣམ་འགྱུར་དང་། ཚིག་ངན་བརྗོད་པ་ལྟ་བུ། བློ་སྦྱོང་སློམ་མཁན་གྱིས། བྱ་བ་ཐམས་ཅད་ལ་སྤྱོད་ཚུལ་རྩ་བ་པོ་ཀོ་ལོང་གི་རིགས་མི་སྟོམ་སྟེ།
དུས་ནམ་ཡང་མ་ཤོར་བར་རྒྱུད་འཇམ་ཞིང་བོག་ཆེ་བ་སོགས་མི་གཞིས་བསྐྱིང་པོར་གནས་དགོས་པར་གསུངས་སོ། པོ་ཏོ་བའི་ཞལ་ནས་ཀྱང་། འོ་སྐོལ་ཆོས་པ་རྣམས་ཆོས་བདག་འཛིན་གྱི་
གཉེན་པོར་མ་སོང་བས། བཟོད་སྲན་ཤའུ་བས་ཆུང་། ཀོ་ལོང་གཙང་བཙན་བས་དམ་པར་གདའ་སྟེ། དེས་ཆོས་ཀྱིས་གོ་མི་ཆོད་པས་ཆོས་བདག་འཛིན་གྱི་གཉེན་པོར་འགྲོ་བ་ཞིག་དགོས་
གསུངས་པ་ལྟ་བུའོ། ཉེར་གཅིག་པ། །ཡུད་ཙམ་པ་མི་བྱ། ཞེས་པས་རང་ཚུགས་བརྟན་པོ་མི་ཟིན་ཏེ་གྲོགས་བཟང་ངན་གྱི་དབང་དུ་ཤོར་ནས་ལུས་ངག་ཡིད་ཀྱི་སྤྱོད་ཚུལ་ཡུད་ཙམ་པ་ཡིས་
འགྱུར་འགྲོ་བ་དེ་འདྲ་མི་བྱ་གསུངས། ཉེར་གཉིས་པ། །འོར་ཆེ་མ་འདོད། ཅེས་པས་གཞན་པ་དྲག་གཞན་མཆོག་དམན་ཀུན་ལ། རང་གིས་ཕན་ཐབས་གང་དྲག་བྱས་པ་ལ་འོར་ཆེ་སྟེ་
བཀའ་དྲིན་ཆེ་ཟེར་བ་ལྟ་བུའི་ངོ་སོ་ཆེ་བའི་ལན་དང་། ལུས་ངག་ཡིད་དང་ལོངས་སྤྱོད་ཀྱིས་དགེ་བའི་བྱ་བ་རང་གིས་ཅི་བགྱིས་པ་ལ་སྙན་གྲགས་དང་། བསྟོད་པ་བསྟི་བཀུར་ཆེན་པོ་འབྱུང་བ་

སོགས་ཀྱི་རེ་བ་བློ་སྦྱོང་ཉམས་སུ་ལེན་པས་མ་འདོད་གསུངས་སོ། །སྙིགས་མ་ལྔ་པོ་བདོ་བ་འདི། །བྱང་ཆུབ་ལམ་དུ་བསྒྱུར་བ་ཡིན། །མན་ངག་བདུད་རྩིའི་སྙིང་པོ་འདི། །གསེར་གླིང་
པ་ནས་བརྒྱུད་པ་ཡིན། ཞེས་གསུངས་ཏེ། དེང་སང་དུས་ངན་པ་སྙིགས་མ་ལྔ་པོ་ཤིན་ཏུ་སྟོབས་ཆེ་ཞིང་བདོ་བ་འདི་ཡང་། ཆོས་གཞན་གྱིས་གློ་བུར་རྐྱེན་ངན་ལམ་དུ་ཁྱེར་ནས་འདུལ་དཀའ་
བའི་སྐབས་འདིར། བདག་གཞན་བརྗེ་བའི་བྱང་ཆུབ་སེམས་བློ་སྦྱོང་ཟབ་མོ་ཉམས་སུ་ལེན་མཁན་ལ་རྐྱེན་ངན་མི་འདོད་པ་ཇི་ཙམ་མང་བ་ཉམས་ལེན་གྱི་གྲོགས་སུ་ཤར་ནས་བྱང་ཆུབ་ལམ་དུ་
བསྒྱུར་ནུས་པ་ཡིན་པས། གཞན་ལ་མེད་པའི་ཁྱད་ཆོས། ཇོ་བོ་བཀའ་གདམས་པའི་བདག་འཛིན་འདུལ་བའི་མན་ངག་ནད་སོས་ཀྱི་སྨན་བཟང་པོ་བདུད་རྩི་ལྟ་བུའི་ཆོས་ཕུང་ཐམས་ཅད་ཀྱི་
སྙིང་པོ་འདི་ནི། ཨ་ཏི་ཤ་ལ་བྱང་ཆུབ་སེམས་ཀྱི་སྦྱོང་བ་ཁྱད་པར་ཅན་སྟོན་པའི་བླ་མ་གསུམ་བཞུགས་པའི་ཡ་གྱལ། གསེར་གླིང་པ་ཆོས་ཀྱི་གྲགས་པ་ནས་བརྒྱུད་པའི་བཀའ་སྲོལ་ཡིན་ཅིང་།
འདིས༔ ཇོ་བོ་རྗེ་ལ་གནང་། དེས་ཐུགས་སྲས་ཀྱི་གཙོ་བོ་འབྲོམ་སྟོན་པ། དེས་དགེ་བའི་བཤེས་གཉེན་པོ་ཏོ་བ་རིན་ཆེན་གསལ། དེས་དགེ་བཤེས་ཤ་ར་བ་ཡོན་ཏན་གྲགས། འདི་ལ་

༄༅། །བཀའ་བབས་ཀྱི་སློབ་མ་བཞི་ལས། བྱང་ཆུབ་སེམས་ཀྱི་བཀའ་བབས་པ་འཆད་ཁ་བ་ཡེ་ཤེས་རྡོ་རྗེ་ལ་གནང་བ་ཡིན་ནོ། སྤོན་སྦྲང་ལས་ཀྱི་འཕྲོ་སད་པས། །
རང་གི་མོས་པ་མང་བའི་རྒྱུས། །སྡུག་བསྔལ་གཏམ་ངན་ཁྲིད་བསད་ནས། །བདག་འཛིན་འདུལ་བའི་གདམས་ངག་ཞུས། །ད་ནི་ཤི་ཡང་མི་འགྱོད་དོ། ཞེས་གསུངས་ཏེ། དགེ་བའི་
བཤེས་གཉེན་ཆེན་པོ་འཆད་ཁ་བ་སྤོན་སྦྲངས་ལས་ཀྱི་འཕྲོ་སད་པས། བདག་འཛིན་འདུལ་བའི་ཆོས་བློ་སྦྱོང་སྒོམ་པ་ལ་རང་གི་མོས་པའི་ཐུགས་དུས་རེས་འགའ་བ་མ་ཡིན་པར་མང་བ་སྙེ་རྒྱུན་
དུ་འབྲུངས་པའི་རྒྱུས། དང་པོ་ཆོས་ཚོལ་བའི་སྐབས་དང་། བར་དུ་ཉམས་སུ་བླངས་པའི་དུས་ཐམས་ཅད་ལ་དཀའ་སྤྱད་མཛད་པའི་སྡུག་བསྔལ་དང་། གཞན་གྱིས་ཚིག་རྩུབ་གཏམ་ངན་
ཐམས་ཅད་ཁྲིད་དུ་བསད་ནས། འདི་ལྷ་བུའི་བདག་འཛིན་འདུལ་བའི་གདམས་ངག་ཞུས་ཏེ་ལེགས་པར་སྦྱངས་པ་ལ་བརྟེན། བདག་བས་གཞན་གཅེས་ཀྱི་བྱང་ཆུབ་སེམས་ཀྱིས་ཐུགས་རྒྱུད་
འབྱོངས་པས། ད་ནི་ཐུགས་དགོངས་ཡོངས་སུ་རྫོགས་པའི་ཕྱིར་དུས་ནམ་ཞིག་ལ་ཤི་ཡང་མི་འགྱོད་དོ། ཅེས་གསུངས་སོ།

།དེ་ཡན་གྱིས་དོན་བདུན་མའི་གཞུང་དོན་རང་ནུས་གང་དཔོག་ལྷག་བསམ་གྱིས་མཚན་བུ་བཏབ་ནས། འདི་ལ། བྱང་ཆུབ་གཞུང་ལམ་དུ་བརྒྱུད་པའི་གདམས་པས་ཁ་སྐོང་མཛད་པ་
འདི་བློ་སྦྱོང་སྒོམ་པའི་གེགས་སེལ་ཤིན་ཏུ་ཕན་པ་འདུག་པས་དེ་ལས་བསྡུ་ན། དེ་ཡང་། ཚེ་གཅིག་བློ་སྦྱོང་སྒོམ་པ་པོའི་སེམས་ལ། གནས་ཁང་སྐྱིད་པོ་དང་། མལ་སྟན་བཟང་པོ།
གཞན་གྱིས་བཀུར་སྟི་སོགས་ཐམས་ཅད་ལས་ལྷག་པ་ཞིག་ཡོང་བར་འདོད་པ་དང་། ཕྱི་མ་ཡང་བདེ་སྐྱིད་ཕུན་སུམ་འཚོགས་པ་འདོད་པ་སོགས་འདོད་ཆུང་ཆོག་ཤེས་ཀྱི་ནོར་བུ་འཕྲོག་པའི་རྣམ
སེམས་ཀྱི་རྣམ་རྟོག་ངན་པ་བྱུང་ན། དེའི་ལན་དུ་རང་ལ་ཤགས་འདེབས་པ་ནི། ཇོ་བོ་གསེར་གླིང་པ་ཆེན་པོས། །ཁྱོད་ཀྱི་གཞིས་ལུགས་འདི་འདྲ་ན། །གནས་མལ་འདི་ཡང་ཡང་རབས་
ཡིན། །བློ་སེམས་འདི་ཡང་བདེ་མོ་ཡིན། གཞན་ཏུ་ཁྲིད་ཀྱིས་སྡུག་སྔན་འདེིས། །དམྱལ་བར་མ་སྐྱེས་ཁ་རྗེ་ཆེ། །བཙོ་སྲེག་མ་མྱོང་ཁ་རྗེ་ཆེ། ཞེས་གསུངས་ཏེ། རང་རྒྱུད་ཆོས་དང
མ་འདྲེས་པའི་ཁྱོད་ཀྱི་གཞིས་ལུགས་ངན་པ་བདག་འཛིན་གྱི་ཁོལ་པོར་གྱུར་པ་འདི་འདྲ་ན། ད་ལྟའི་སྡོད་གནས་མལ་ས་ཞིག་སྙིང་པ་འདིའང་ཡང་རབས་ཡིན་ཅིང་། རྣམ་རྟོག་ངན་གོམས་ཀྱི

སོ་གསུམ་

༄༅། །དབང་དུ་སོང་བའི་སེམས་འདི་ཡང་བདག་འཛིན་གདོན་གྱིས་དེ་སྟེ་མ་སྨྱོ་བར་ཐ་མལ་དུ་གནས་པ་བདེ་མོ་ཡིན་པ་མ་ཟད། གཞན་དུ་ཁྲིད་ཀྱིས་དགེ་བ་བྱེད་པ་ལ་
དཀའ་ཐུབ་མི་ནུས་པར་མི་དགེ་བའི་ལས་ལ་སྡུག་སྲན་ཆེ་བ་འདིས་འབྲས་བུ་དམྱལ་བར་ད་དུང་མ་སྐྱེས་པ་ཁ་རྗེ་ཆེ་བ་དང་། དངོས་སུ་དམྱལ་བའི་ལས་མཁན་ཡོང་སྟེ་བཙོ་སྲེག་གི་སྡུག་བསྔལ་
མ་མྱོང་བ་ཁ་རྗེ་ཆེ་བ་ཡིན་ཞེས་རང་གིས་རང་ལ་ཁྲེལ་བདས་དགོས་གསུངས་སོ། དེ་བཞིན་དུ་གསེར་གླིང་པས། །གཞན་ཡང་འཇིགས་པ་རབ་བསམ་སྟེ། །བདག་ལ་ཁྲེལ་བདས་ཆེན་པོ་
བྱ། །ལྟོ་ལ་གྲོང་བསྐུར་དཀའ་ཐུབ་བྱ། །གོས་ལ་གྲོང་བསྐུར་དམན་ཆ་བླང་། །བདེ་སྡུག་ཁྲིད་བསད་གཉེན་པོ་བསྒོམ། ཞེས་གསུངས་པ་ནི་གོ་སླའོ། ཡང་བློ་སྦྱོང་གི་ཆོས་ནི། །གཅིག་
ཕུར་འདུག་ན་སྐྱོ་རོགས་ཡིན། །ན་བའི་ཚེ་ན་ནད་གཡོག་ཡིན། ཅེས་པའང་ཡིད་སྐྱོ་བ་དྲག་པོས་གདུང་བ་སོགས་ཏུ་ཐུག་པའི་ཚེ་འཇིག་རྟེན་པའི་གྲོགས་པོ་ལ་ཡིད་ལྟོས་ཀྱང་རེ་བ་བཞིན་ཕན་
བྱེད་པ་དཀའ་ཡང་། བླ་མ་ཆགས་མེད་ཀྱིས། བྱང་ཆུབ་སེམས་ནི་རྟག་ཏུ་བདེ་བའི་རྒྱུ། གསུངས་པ་བཞིན་བློ་སྦྱོང་ནི་རང་གཅིག་པུར་གནས་པའི་ཚེ་སྐྱོ་རོགས་དང་། དེ་བཞིན་དུ་ན་ཚ་

65

སོགས་ཉམ་ང་བའི་དུས་སུ་ནད་གཡོག་སོགས་རེ་བ་བཞིན་ཕན་བྱེད་པ་རྙེད་པར་དཀའ་ཡང་བྱང་ཆུབ་སེམས་བློ་སྦྱོང་གི་གྲོགས་དང་མ་བྲལ་ན་ཉིན་མཚན་ཀུན་ཏུ་སྐྱོང་བའི་ནད་གཡོག་ཆེན་པོ་དང་།
གཏན་བདེའི་ཕན་པ་རྒྱ་ཆེན་པོ་འབྱུང་བས་གཞན་ལ་རེ་བ་དང་ཡུས་མི་དགོས་པའི་དོན་ནོ། ཡང་གསེར་གླིང་པས་ཇོ་བོ་རྗེ་ལ་ཁྲིད་ཀྱིས་དུས་སླེབས་མར་མཐར་འཁོབ་འདུལ་བ་ལ་གདམས་ངག
འདི་རྣམས་དགོས་གསུངས་ཏེ། །རྟོག་པ་ཐམས་ཅད་འབུར་འཇོམས་ཏེ། །གཉེན་པོ་ཐམས་ཅད་བཙོམ་བརྟེག་ཡིན། །འདུན་མ་ཐམས་ཅད་ཅིག་དྲིལ་ཏེ། །ལམ་རྣམས་ཐམས་ཅད་
གཅིག་ཆོད་ཡིན། །གཉེན་པོ་རྣམ་བྱང་ཆོས་བཞི་སྟེ། །མཐའ་འཁོབ་འདུལ་ན་དགོས་པ་ཡིན། །འཁོར་ངན་ལོག་སྒྲུབ་བཟོད་པ་ལ། །སྙིགས་མའི་དུས་སུ་མཁོ་བ་ཡིན། ཅེས་པས་ཉོན་
མོངས་སོགས་ཀྱི་རྟོག་པ་སྐྱེས་མ་ཐག་འབུར་འཇོམས་དང་། སྡང་བྱའི་ཐོག་ཏུ་གཉེན་པོ་འཕྲལ་དུ་བཙོམ་བརྟེག་དང་། ལམ་ཐམས་ཅད་བདག་འཛིན་འདུལ་བའི་ཆེད་དུ་ཅིག་དྲིལ་དང་།
བདག་འཛིན་ཐུལ་ན་ས་ལམ་ཅིག་ཆོད་ཡིན་པས་དེ་བཞི་ལ་རྣམ་བྱང་ཕྱོགས་ཀྱི་གཉེན་པོ་ཐམས་ཅད་འདུ་བ་ཡིན་ནོ། ཡང་། །རྐྱེན་ངན་དགེ་བའི་བཤེས་གཉེན་ཡིན། །འདྲེ་གདོན་རྒྱལ་བའི་

66

ཤོ་བཞི

༄༅། །སྤྲུལ་པ་ཡིན། །ན་ཚ་སྡིག་སྒྲིབ་ཕྱུགས་ཤིང་ཡིན། །སྡུག་བསྔལ་ཆོས་ཉིད་ཀྱི་ཡོ་ལངས་ཡིན། །ཀུན་ནས་ཉོན་མོངས་ཆོས་བཞི་སྟེ། །མཐའ་འཁོབ་
འདུལ༔ །འཁོར་ངན་ལོག་སྒྲུབ༔ །སྙིགས་མའི་དུས་སུ༔ ཞེས་གསུངས་ཏེ། རྐྱེན་ངན་དང་། འདྲེ་གདོན། ན་ཚ། སྡུག་བསྔལ་སྟེ་ཀུན་ནས་ཉོན་མོངས་ཀྱི་ཆོས་བཞི་སྤྱང་ས་མི་
དགོས་པར་དགེ་བའི་བཤེས་གཉེན་སོགས་དེ་བཞིན་ཐར་པའི་གྲོགས་ཡིན་པར་ངོ་སྤྲོད་པའོ། །སྐྱིད་ཀྱི་གཤའ་གདོན་ཆེན་པོ་ཡིན། །སྡུག་གི་མཛུག་སྟུད་ཆེན་པོ་ཡིན། །མི་མཁོ་ཞོགས་ནི་འདོད་
ཐོག་ཡིན། །ལྟས་ངན་གཡང་དུ་ལེན་པ་ཡིན། །གཉེན་པོ་ལོག་གནོན་གྱི་ཆོས་བཞི་སྟེ། །མཐའ་འཁོབ༔ །འཁོར་ངན༔ །སྙིགས་མའི༔ ཞེས་གསུངས་ཏེ། ལུས་སེམས་སྐྱིད་པ་
བྱུང་ན་འདིས་མཚོན་བདེ་སྐྱིད་ཐམས་ཅད་འགྲོ་ལ་གཏོང་སླམ་པ་དང་། སྐྱིད་པའི་རྟོག་པ་དེ་ཉིད་ཀྱི་ངོ་བོ་སྟོང་ཉིད་དུ་རྩལ་སྦྱང་བས། བདེ་སྐྱིད་ལ་ཆགས་ཞེན་ང་རྒྱལ་སོགས་ཉོན་མོངས་ཀྱི་རྟོག་
པ་སྐྱེས་པ་གཉའ་གནོན་པ་ཡིན་ནོ། དེ་བཞིན་རང་ལ་སྡུག་བསྔལ་བྱུང་ན་སེམས་ཅན་ཀུན་གྱི་སྡུག་བསྔལ་ལེན་ནས་རང་གི་སྡུག་བསྔལ་གྱི་ཐོག་ཏུ་སྤྱུངས། བདག་གིས་སྡུག་བསྔལ་མྱོང་བ་

67

འདིས་སེམས་ཅན་ཐམས་ཅད་སྡུག་བསྔལ་གྱི་འདམ་དུ་བྱིང་བའི་གོ་ཆོད་ནས་དེ་དག་བདེ་བ་དང་ལྡན་པར་གྱུར་ཅིག་བསམ་ཞིང་སྡུག་བསྔལ་གྱི་རང་ངོ་བདེན་པས་སྟོང་པའི་ཀློང་དུ་མཉམ་པར་
འཇོག་ཅིང་རྩལ་སྦྱང་པ་ནི་སྡུག་གི་མཛུག་སྟུད་པ་ཡིན་ཅིང་། དེ་བཞིན་དུ་མི་ཁ་གཏམ་ངན་དཔྲ་གྲོད་སོགས་མི་མཁོ་ཞོགས་རང་ལ་གང་བྱུང་ཡང་། བདག་འཛིན་གྱི་འཚང་ཕུད། གཅེས་འཛིན་
རེ་དོགས་ཀྱི་རྒྱུད་བྲལ་བ་ཡིན་པས་བློ་སྦྱོང་སྒོམ་པའི་གྲོགས་འདོད་ཐོག་བྱུང་བ་ཡིན་བསམ་ནས་ལམ་དུ་འཁྱེར། མི་འདོད་པའི་ན་ཚ་ངན་པ། ཉོན་མོངས་དྲག་པོ། ལྷ་འདྲེས་ཆེ་འཕྲུལ།
བྱད་ཁ་ཕུར་ཁ་སོགས་ལྟས་ངན་གྱི་རིགས་ཅི་བྱུང་ཡང་བློ་སྦྱོང་སྒོམ་པའི་གྲོགས་དང་གཡང་དུ་ལེན་པ་ཡིན་པས་འདི་དག་ནི་གཉེན་པོ་གཞན་གྱིས་མ་ཐུབ་པའི་ལོག་གནོན་གྱི་ཆོས་བཞིའོ།
ཡང་། །བདག་ནི་སྐྱོན་གྱི་རྩ་བ་སྟེ། །རྒྱངས་ཀྱིས་བསྐྱུར་བའི་ཆོས་ཤིག་ཡིན། །གཞན་ནི་ཡོན་ཏན་གྱི་འབྱུང་ཁུངས་ཏེ། །ཅངས་ཏེ་ལེན་པའི་ཆོས་ཤིག་ཡིན། །གཉེན་པོ་མཛུག་སྟུད་
ཀྱི་ཆོས་གཉིས་ཏེ། །མཐའ་འཁོབ་འདུལ་ན་དགོས་པ་ཡིན། །འཁོར་ངན་ལོག་སྒྲུབ་བཟློག་པ་ནི། །སྙིགས་མའི་དུས་སུ་མཁོ་བ་ཡིན། ཞེས་གསུངས་ཏེ། བདག་ནི་ལས་ཉོན་གྱི་རྩ་བ་

68

སོ་ལྔ་

༄༅། །དང་སྡུག་བསྔལ་གྱི་རྟེན་གཞི་ཡིན་པས། རང་ལ་གཅེས་པར་འཛིན་པ་དོར་ནས། གཞན་སེམས་ཅན་ནི། སངས་རྒྱས་ཀྱི་གོ་འཕང་སོགས་གནས་སྐབས་དང་
མཐར་ཐུག་གི་ཕན་བདེའི་འབྱུང་ཁུངས་ཡིན་པས་དང་དུ་ལེན་པ་སྟེ། དེ་ལྟར་བླང་དོར་གཉིས་པོ་ལ་གཉེན་པོ་ཐམས་ཅད་འདུ་བ་ཡིན་ནོ། ཡང་། །ལོག་ཅེར་ལོག་ལ་ཅེར་ཅེར་ལྟོས། །ཤིག
གི་ཤིག་ལ་འབོལ་ལེ་ཞོག །དེས་ནི་མི་འཆིང་གྲོལ་བར་འགྱུར། ཅེས་གསུངས་ཏེ། སེམས་ཕྱི་རོལ་དུ་མི་གཡེངས་བར་ཁ་ནང་དུ་ལོག་ནས་གཟུང་འཛིན་སྤྱངས་པའི་ཆོས་དབྱིངས་སྤྲོས
བྲལ་གྱི་ངང་དུ་ཤེས་པ་གསལ་ལ་རྟོག་པ་མེད་པར་འབོལ་ལེ་ཤིག་གེར་བཅས་བཅོས་སོགས་འཛིན་པ་ཞིག་ནས་གློད་ལ་བཞག དེས་ནི་འཁོར་བས་མི་འཆིང་བར་ཉོན་མོངས་ཡེ་ཤེས་སུ་གྲོལ
བར་འགྱུར་རོ་གསུངས་སོ།། ༈ །བློ་སྦྱོང་ཉམས་ལེན་ལ་ཚེ་གཅིག་ཏུ་བསྟེན་པའི་ཕན་ཡོན་ནི། ལུས་ཀྱི་ནད་གདོན་དང་སྡིག་སྒྲིབ་ཐམས་ཅད་ཟད་པར་འགྱུར་བ་དང་། བར་ཆད་དངོས་གྲུབ
ཏུ་འགྱུར་ཞིང་ལྷ་འདྲེ་མི་རྣམས་བྱམས་པ་དང་སྙན་པའི་གྲགས་པ་ཕྱོགས་ཀུན་ལ་འཕེལ་ཞིང་གྲོགས་འཁོར་ཟས་ནོར་འདུ་བ་དང་། ལུས་ལ་བདེ་བ། ངག་ལ་ནུས་པ། སེམས་ལ་རྟོགས་པ

69

འབར་བ་དང་། སེམས་ཅན་གང་གིས་མཐོང་བ་ལ་བྱིན་རླབས་འཇུག་ཅིང་དེ་དག་གི་ལས་ཉོན་གྱི་སྒྲིབ་པ་བྱང་བར་འགྱུར་བ་དང་། མཐར་ཐུག་བྱང་ཆེན་ཐོབ་པ་སོགས་ཕན་ཡོན་ཚད་མེད་པར
གསུངས་སོ། ཇོ་བློ་གྲོས་མཐའ་ཡས་ཀྱི་རྒྱས་འགྲེལ་ལས་ཀྱང་། །མདོ་སྔགས་ལམ་གྱི་རྩ་བ་སྟེ། །དམ་ཆོས་ཀུན་གྱི་སྙིང་པོའི་བཅུད། །ཟབ་ཅིང་ཉམས་སུ་བླང་བདེ་བ། །ཁྲིད་རྩུལ་ཀུན
ལས་ རྨད་དུ་བྱུང་། །ཟབ་ཆོས་འདི་འདྲ་ཐོས་པ་དཀའ། །ཐོས་ནས་ཉམས་སུ་ལེན་པ་དཀའ། །འདི་སྦྱོད་བསོད་ནམས་ནོར་ལྡན་པ། །དེང་སང་ས་སྙིང་གསེར་བཞིན་དཀོན། ཅེས་བསྔགས
བརྗོད་མཛད་པ་བཞིན་ཟབ་ཆོས་འདི་ཡི་ཁྲིད་ལུང་ཙམ་ཐོབ་ནའང་བསྐལ་པ་བཟང་པོར་འགྱུར་བ་གདོན་མི་ཟ་བས་དེ་ལྟར་བསྟེན་པ་བསྐྱེད་དོ། །བདག་ནི་སྨོམ་གསུམ་ནོར་བུའི་རྒྱན་གླུབ
ཀྱང་། །རང་སེམས་ཉོན་མོངས་ཛག་ལ་འཚོར་འདེིས་མཐུས། །ཁ་ནས་ནེ་ཙོས་མ་ཏེའི་དཔེ་བཞིན་གྱིས། །ཟབ་ཆོས་བློ་སྦྱོང་ཚུང་ཟད་མཆན་གྱིས་ཕྱེས། །ལེགས་བྱས་རིན་ཆེན་གཡུར་རྩུ
རྒྱུན་གྱིས། །མཐའ་ཡས་འགྲོ་བའི་སྡུག་བསྔལ་ཚ་གདུངས་སེལ། །སྣང་ནས་སྣང་བའི་མཐར་ཐུག་བཙོམ་ལྡན་གྱི། །གོ་འཕང་དམ་པར་ཡིད་ཙམ་རྒྱལ་གྱུར་ཅིག །ཅེས་བློ་སྦྱོང་དོན་བདུན

70

༄༅། །མའི་མཆན་འགྲེལ་མདོར་བསྡུས་སྡུག་བསྔལ་མུན་སེལ་ཞེས་བྱ་བ་འདི། བྱང་ཆུབ་གཞུང་ལམ་གྱི་ཁྲིད་ལུང་ཐོབ་པ་ཡིན་སྐབས། དེའི་རྩ་བའི་འགྲོས་དང་བསྟུན༑ དམ་པའི་གསུངས་གཞན་གྱིས་ཀྱང་བརྒྱན། གཙོ་བོར་རང་གིས་གོ་སླ་རྣམས་དྲན་གསོར་དམིགས་ཏེ། བྱང་ཆུབ་ཏུ་སེམས་བསྐྱེད་པའི་གྲལ་མཐར་འཁོད་ཅིང་། ཀཿཐོག་ཀྲའི་རྗེས་འཇུག་གི་རྟགས་ཙམ་འཆང་བ་ཀརྨ་ཕྲིན་ལས་པས། སྨོན་ཆེན་བྱང་གླིང་རྒྱལ་ཁབ་ནས་བྲིས་པའི་དགེ་བས། འཇིག་རྟེན་ཀུན་ཏུ་ནད་མུག་མཚོན་འཁྲུག་སོགས་སྡུག་བསྔལ་གྱི་རྒྱུ་དང་འབྲས་བུ་མཐའ་དག་ལས་ཡོངས་སུ་གྲོལ་ཞིང་ཕན་བདེའི་དཔལ་དམ་པར་དབང་འབྱོར་བ་དང་། རྡོ་བོ་བཀའ་གདམས་པའི་སྐྱེན་བརྒྱུད་ཐབ་ཆོས་བློ་སྦྱོང་གི་གདམས་པའི་ཉི་གཞོན་ཕྱོགས་ཀུན་ཏུ་འབར་བར་གྱུར་ཅིག།།

།།རིག་འཛིན་མཁའ་འགྲོས་དཔར་བསྐྲུན་གྱི་ཁུར་བླངས་པ་དགེ་ལེགས་འཕེལ།

Publishing finished
in January 2023 by Pulsio
Publisher Number: 4023
Legal Deposit: January 2023
Printed in Bulgaria